MESSAGES FROM A DOCTOR
IN THE
FOURTH DIMENSION
Volume 3

Dr Karl Nowotny

MESSAGES FROM A DOCTOR IN THE FOURTH DIMENSION

Volume 3
by
Dr Karl Nowotny

Tudor Press (London),
27 Old Gloucester Street,
London WC1N 3XX

Copyright 1993 by Dr. Karl Nowotny Foundation e.V.(English edition)

First published under the title *Mediale Schriften* in Germany 1972
This edition 1993
Translated by Olga Van Oppens and Sieglinde Bader.

Permission for reproduction only with the express
written authority from Dr. Karl Nowotny Foundation e.V.,
Reichenhaller Strasse 69, D-8230, Bad Reichenhall 4,
Germany.

Cover: Hans Neubert, D-8121 Paehl

ISBN 1 874514 09 7

Printed and bound in Great Britain by the Longdunn Press Ltd, Barton
Manor, St Philips, Bristol BS2 ORL.

Contents

Foreword by Sir George Trevelyan.	9
How it Began.	11
The purpose of the messages.	14
Community consciousness as a basis for material and spiritual progress. The danger of inter-marriage between people of civilised and primitive societies.	17
The incorrect interpretation of the value of sexual intercourse. Its dangers and necessary clarification.	20
The effects of abnormal unions and methods of healing the resultant degeneracies. The other-worldly point of view on the termination of pregnancies.	23
Inherited degeneracies. Epilepsy, multiple sclerosis and their causes.	26
A doctor's opinion of human modes of behaviour based on general norms in relation to individual personality.	30
Reactions and their importance in a medical examination and the establishment of a perfect diagnosis.	33
Repercussions of emotional impressions. Common sense.	36
Correct deliberation the way to knowledge and wisdom. Memory, the basis for the spirit entity's activity. Imagination, the mirror image of past existence in the world beyond.	40
The prevailing theory about heredity is an obstacle to the establishment of truth.	43
Useful and useless knowledge. The necessity of changing the social order. The unequal distribution of possessions is justified.	46
Overestimation of matter is caused by the non-fulfilment of the blueprint brought to earth. Clairvoyance a mediumistic ability.	50

The philosophy of life of the individual in relation to the community. The interrelationship of spirit and soul.	53
Incorrect interpretation of technical progress. Consequences of inventions and research conducted without feeling.	56
The soul is the link to the spirit world. It is hampered by the wrong concept of life and death. Advice on curing abnormal emotional and mental attitudes.	59
The cultivation of art is a significant component of a healthy philosophy of life. Definition of "art."	62
Attitude to life is not a product of philosophical planning, but rather a style of living and adaption of the given fundamentals. The error of religions.	65
Some thoughts about making a living. The community and society.	67
Personal judgement, courage and self-confidence as the basis for re-adjusting to a sound attitude to life.	70
The value and advantage of knowledge and wisdom.	73
The assessment of human qualities in the study of character. A justifiable and exaggerated desire to gain recognition.	76
The courage to face the truth and the hampering effect of one's upbringing and environment.	78
Living together in the family.	81
Marriage and family not always necessary for the fulfilment of the blueprint.	85
The search for life's blueprint is not the correct choice of a career. The end of life not synonymous with attaining one's goal.	88
Moral and legal obligation.	91
Poverty and wealth as bases for the achievement of life's tasks.	93
The possibility of making good a programme that has gone wrong. Sound and abnormal imagination. Spiritualism is not a game.	96
Some basic rules for those seeking progress and truth. The boundaries between egotism and altruism.	99

Spiritual values are never lost. The difference between "goodness" and "loving kindness".	102
The purpose of eternal laws is spiritual perfection. "Evil" as opposed to "goodness". The development of mankind as seen from the other world.	104
The perfect human being does not exist. The lie is an attribute of civilisation. Spiritual work depends on the physical disposition.	108
Prominent qualities indicate the blueprint. What has been mastered cannot be lost.	111
Aimless wandering of certain spirit entities. Ways of maintaining spiritual contact between the incarnate and discarnate worlds.	114
The course of incarnation.	117
The necessary interdependence between this world and the next.	119
Depressions brought on by lack of courage to face oneself and their treatment.	122
Hysteria, how to recognise and treat it. Negative and positive autosuggestion.	125

Foreword

WHILST I am not a Spiritualist, I have no doubt that after physical death the mind, memory, personality and individuality remain. I am equally as certain that under the right conditions spiritual beings can manifest, and, now blessed with a wider breadth of vision, can communicate teachings which are of vital importance to mankind. There is probably nothing new in the notion of communication with the next world. Indeed, the process by which it operates is as old as mankind.

Now there is no doubt whatsoever that the human brain consists of two parts. The masculine is responsible for the build-up of a great technological civilisation. Meanwhile, the right half, which is feminine, is intuitive, able to grasp the living one-ness of things and comprehend the spiritual world. What an adventure awaits all on entry into this higher dimension!

Whilst I did not know Dr Karl Nowotny when he was on earth, I am more than happy to endorse the teachings which he has communicated from the next realm. Controversial? Yes, sometimes they are. But I view this as a decided asset. Honest controversy is the means by which debate is widened and deepened. This should be welcomed. We have nothing to fear but much to gain from exploring others' views.

The teachings from Dr Nowotny bear, I believe, a hallmark of sincerity. They "feel" right in a way which is difficult to put into words.

Only now, after a long period of evolution, is mankind beginning to awake. This is the excitement of our time as we enter the much-heralded Aquarian Age.

In the last 2,000 years of the Piscean Age it was necessary to build up the structure of Western civilisation. One of the greatest sadnesses is that so many scientists turned away from spiritual truths and, blinded by rampant materialism, refused to accept anything that was not demonstrable and repeatable in laboratory experiments.

However, even this is starting to change. Generally speaking, there is an awakening to the Spirit, a realisation than man is more than flesh and bones, that he is motivated by a spiritual force. Indeed, without this vital force, life itself would fail to operate.

Dr Nowotny casts new light on a series of situations and problems. Often — and with some justification — the charge is made that spiritual messages are banal, that they add nothing new to the sum total of human knowledge and endeavour.

This claim most certainly cannot be made about Dr Nowotny. His teachings are both thought provoking and mind expanding. From his new vantage point he is able to offer advice which is both sensible and practical.

Truly is change upon us all. I see it all around me in so many ways. At least, mankind has come to the rightful realisation that the earth, for example, is a living, breathing entity, one with whom we must work in love, harmony and friendship.

Spiritual teachings have a vital part to play in spreading this message, emphasising as they often do, the essential one-ness of all life. Truly is every one — and every thing — interconnected.

Dr Nowotny's teachings are both important and interesting. It is for this reason I have no hesitation whatsoever in recommending them, and hope they reach the widest possible audience.

Sir George Trevelyan

How it began

DR KARL NOWOTNY, a specialist in neurology and one of the foremost representatives of individual psychology, died on April 18, 1965.

Long before this, I visited him as a patient. Time and again over the years I had occasion to appreciate his humanity and outstanding personality. I had boundless confidence, respect and admiration for him, both as a person and as a doctor. He had advice and help for every situation and gave courage and strength when sorrow and worry made life seem unbearable. At that time I had no idea a contact that would vastly exceed our medical friendship would unite me with him one day on a psychic theme. I will explain briefly how this came about.

Two days before he died, I had a dream. A figure stood before me and spoke three words, "Nowotny is dying." I was shocked by this unequivocal communication, but could not believe it because the day before, he told me he would spend the Easter holidays in his country house. Although Dr Nowotny had been ailing for some time, there was no reason for concern. Nevertheless, I could not forget the dream. On April 19 — the day after his death — I took courage and tried to reach him by phone. There was no reply that day — or the next. Something was obviously very wrong. By the time I had a reply from his home in Vienna on the 21st, I was not at all surprised by the news.

Deeply moved, I told a dear friend who was visiting me about my vision and the prediction. For many years she had been receiving messages through a good medium from a spirit entity who, in his earthly life, had been a cleric and close friend of her husband. Her medium was due in Vienna in the summer to continue working with her. She offered to introduce me to her to see whether "Victor," the cleric, could bring us Dr Nowotny. I had always refused to have anything to do with Spiritualism, but this time agreed without hesitation.

The medium, Bertha, had barely entered my home when Dr Nowotny came through. I must add that the medium had no idea what I wanted and never knew him. Bertha is a speaking medium who works while fully conscious; she does not go into trance. Anxiously,

MESSAGES FROM A DOCTOR IN THE FOURTH DIMENSION

I waited for concrete evidence that I was not being hoaxed and deceived. My friend who brought the medium took this message in shorthand so I am able to reproduce it word for word:

"I purposely come for only a short while. I do not come because I have been summoned, but because I have the desire to make a brief visit.

"It will be a long time before we meet here. This is why one should never think about the departure from the material world, but always only of life and the obligation to do one's duty so one can pass through the high portals into the dazzlingly radiant hall with a clear conscience.

"People live in the dark; they do not want to see clearly. But when we have passed through the door, we are enlightened and are happy that life on earth is behind us. There is a world beyond. For me, it is this world. Oh, how short human life is! It is over so quickly. One must be strong and not falter in one's plans, not succumb to earthly desires, but be happy, always seeing the good side of things. Sadness makes us weak and weary for every type of work.

"I can only say I am content and do not regret I had to terminate my life. I had many good friends. I am happy to have had them."

In answer to my question, "What are you doing now, doctor?" came the reply: "I have as much to do as when I was alive. Many people come and want my advice, but they don't follow it. I have given a lot of people encouragement and tried to strengthen them. They pay no attention after they have left me. They are like children leaving school. They don't think about the lesson and forget what they have learned."

If his first words encouraged me to think that everything was in order, the last sentence convinced me completely because these were the exact ones he often used to round off his lectures at his adult evening classes.

Subsequently, I made several trips to Budapest and the medium Bertha in order to maintain contact and to receive more reassuring messages. It was a great success, but the wish for constant contact grew steadily stronger. Through the medium, I asked Dr Nowotny if he would not try to write with my hand, as I knew about automatic writing.

In October 1966, we tried this for the first time. After two days, I could receive messages, albeit slowly, without the medium. The writing grew steadily stronger and faster. In April 1967, I began this work.

The first volume comprised 116 pages of manuscript. Dr Nowotny said much more was to follow. The text is transcribed word for word from the manuscript.

I conclude with Dr Nowotny's wish, "May this work be an incentive for doctors and all interested readers to guide people along the right path, to show them the value of a good philosophy of life and give them peace and confidence."

The medium Grete

Introduction

The purpose of the messages

MY observations about illnesses of the soul are clearly expressed and by no means claim to be academic dissertations. They should help to give many people an insight and a closer understanding of the subject. Medical aid is rarely sought and actually available in cases of emotional illnesses. My writings may cause you to think about the benefits of a healthy life-style as well as the results of negative influences on the spirit and soul.

Doctors still have a lot to learn in order to dominate this subject and ensure that every case is infallibly diagnosed. I cannot incorporate medical lectures into these messages. The average reader would not understand them. My good intentions, which accompany them, would be lost.

When medical practitioners and students take my statements for granted, and freely admit that they do so, a publisher with the courage to present my scientific writings from the world beyond will be found. As I have already said, this will be in the not too distant future. Until then I will assist all individual cases brought to my attention and secretly ensure that the mistakes that still persist in some aspects of medicine do not cause too much damage.

Much to my joy and gratification I have established that since my departure from the material world and the publication of my messages as well as my work with my medium, a number of prominent doctors have changed their views and now follow my basic teachings. None of them has suffered bad results. My diagnoses have proved correct and the recommended treatments been successful.

The fact that radical changes cannot be introduced overnight is both right and understandable. Every process takes time. Such decisive transformations must be soundly established and guided.

Do not, therefore, consider my writings a directive to throw overboard today's practices, which have had good results. Rather make appropriate experiments with individual cases and in this way come to the gradual conviction that my information is correct.

I think this has to be mentioned because I have sensed that several doctors expected to extract profound scientific explanations from my writings. I have promised to give these and will keep my promise, but not in this series of books. My observations tell me much more than you, dear reader, can imagine. I always tried to encourage people with whom I had dealings of any kind to reflect on a given topic and come to a personal conclusion.

It is absolutely amazing how I have witnessed this among the relatively few people who read my first books of messages. None of them has laid them aside without reflection. This is not intended as publicity for my books, which will certainly afford many, many people happiness and contentment. I only want to point out and underline the purpose of my work.

I also want to make it clear that not every problem and every aspect of vital and necessary information has been exhaustively dealt with.

You tend to forget too easily whatever has not been achieved and adopted through personal endeavour.

The transformation of character and the embodiment of a sound philosophy of life must be a personal discovery and attainment. This is not achieved through sensational communications about otherworldly circumstances and conditions which human intellect cannot understand in any case.

The duties and responsibilities of the universe are divided and allotted according to specific laws. Therefore a human being will never be blessed with the abilities and powers which those in the world beyond achieve once they have found the path.

It is easy to make a simple comparison if you really wish to understand the purpose of trying to make progress: an earthly person sees a goal and strives with all his might to attain it. In order to do so, he must be totally aware of all the means at his disposal and use them in order to ensure his gradual advance towards this goal. Nobody can become the head of a government without having been a lowly helper and follower of great predecessors. Of course this does not apply to those who have seized power unconstitutionally.

Far greater and loftier qualities are required to understand the

MESSAGES FROM A DOCTOR IN THE FOURTH DIMENSION

powers and circumstances in the other-worldly sphere in their total magnitude and splendour. How much more intensely must man learn to work at perfecting himself before he is allowed to move into the highest regions.

In one of my earlier messages I drew attention to the fact that it is not essential to believe in life after death and a return to earthly existence. It is only important that man feels the urge to higher development within himself during his brief sojourn in the material world.

That I nevertheless speak about the links with the world beyond and stress the importance of believing in them is rooted in the fact that it gives an aspirant unbelievable comfort to realise that he can receive help. It is there for everybody to enjoy. This knowledge spares great disappointment, gives peace and contentment and expedites progress on the upward path far more rapidly than the greatest endeavour which is fraught with disbelief and mistakes.

My wise pupils who happily accept my help can vouch for this. But perhaps the time is not yet right and requires proof positive to invalidate the stubborn rejection of learned society.

Today I want to speak somewhat more generally about the problems posed by my work from my point of view. It may serve to clarify all kinds of doubts. In this series of messages I will examine special areas which are important for a sound approach to life and, as I see it, are to be judged a little differently from the way they are in the material world.

Community consciousness as a basis for material and spiritual progress. The danger of inter-marriage between people of civilised and primitive societies.

IT is necessary to keep pointing out that man alone cannot determine his destiny. He is subject to eternal laws which demand absolute logical consistency in all matters and cannot evade them.

In earthly life, many people think that the responsibilities and rules which the masses take for granted and have to observe do not apply to them, the privileged few.

Consider the measures adopted for the so-called free life. Do not believe that whoever wishes to can step out of line when it comes to social and civil fundamentals. They must apply to everybody and offer all the same possibility of organising his life in a systematic way.

It is, therefore, quite wrong that the greatest champions of the natural sciences - and I refer to chemistry and physics - seek to make progress in their personal, restricted fields while completely ignoring the effects of their experiments on their fellow men; experiments which in many instances are mortally dangerous. We consider such mistakes, which they undoubtedly are from the human point of view, crimes. Many a scholar — of course I only refer to someone who is aware of the results of his experiments — realises when he crosses over into the world beyond what he has done and how he has disregarded the divine laws.

No material progress should be detrimental to mankind. Such progress will one day be condemned to regression or downfall. It was not without reason that the ancient Egyptian kingdom was destroyed by energies from other-worldly realms. The folly of the great scholars of those days drove them far beyond their allotted boundaries. Negative influences from the spiritual spheres tried to anticipate developments which were programmed for a much later period in time. Bringing them forward would have provoked the greatest calamities.

The danger was not confined to ancient Egyptian times. It is still present today. All scholars and advanced masters of technology should always bear this in mind. Their great discoveries which harm human welfare are miniscule achievements. What I really mean is they are not achievements at all because honour and acclaim count for nothing in the world beyond and eternal life. There only a very limited number of scientists will be allowed to make use of their success attained on earth. They are those who placed their overwhelming knowledge at the service of the community.

Community life in the material world requires universally valid laws and institutions if mankind is to make sound progress. This is why civilisation - a concept based on such institutions - has been created and developed. But it is a mistake to imagine that the form in which it exists on one side of the globe can be transmitted to all other remaining areas. Just as a child develops slowly and is not able to use all the achievements of civilisation from birth, so in the main are the different stages of spiritual maturity and development.

All great men in the civilised world should adopt this viewpoint and not overshoot the mark so brutally, if I may use this expression.

One cannot force a way of life onto a primitive society; a way of life far beyond its comprehension. But one service can be rendered. This is my underlying theme today: the instillation of a sense of community consciousness, a love of cleanliness, and tidiness and instruction in health care. Development aid volunteers and doctors have the duty of giving help to underdeveloped nations, to assist them to advance so that a healthier way of life enables them to bring about normal mental achievements. Only the foundations should be provided because no rung up the ladder of development may be omitted if progress is to be made.

Technical achievements that have not been produced in the country itself, that have not been created by indigenous scholars and persons with a calling retard the development process because they do not help to discover the true objective of human life, but only provide the drive for material advantage and a so-called progressive life style. They will not be appreciated. All these things established as benefits will inevitably be left to rot. The inhabitants of such countries will then be accused of ingratitude. If you ask me, I think they are right in opposing such measures as soon as they realise that money alone does not represent happiness.

These people, poor in the eyes of the civilised world, should only receive medical aid. In underdeveloped nations there are always advanced people who have been designated as mediators to serve the community without forcing them into an unfamiliar and strange way of life. There have been several such great men who have traded their lives in the civilised world for an arduous but extremely happy life in the wilderness. Every one of them accomplished great deeds and achieved goals way above all expectations. They were all protected by good spirits and rank as outstanding role-models in the history of medicine.

Why has it been considered necessary to undermine the good idea of development aid because of a thirst for power and a totally false drive for personal prestige? To abuse this concept for material gain and dominate poor, tormented fellow men?

Gradually, very gradually, the civilised world is beginning to see the error of its ways, which have only had negative results.

"So shalt thou dwell in the land and verily thou shalt be fed" is a wise maxim, although it cannot be denied that mankind would greatly benefit from a knowledge of the world from various angles. A one-sided point of view is not ideal. The same principle in the same form does not apply to two people.

This brings me to a subject that will interest neurologists and psychiatrists: illnesses brought from foreign shores to more developed countries resulting from the inter-marriage of civilised and primitive peoples. They are a great danger for the general health of a country.

As we know, in all spheres the foreign and the unknown take precedence over the habitual and the everyday. This also applies to lifestyles, manners and customs.

In the same way that the civilised world forces its attainments on primitive nations so these in return unwittingly introduce their customs and habits to civilised people. Either greatly impressed or purely for sensational reasons, they believe they have to emulate them and make them a part of their daily life.

There is no need to explain how absurd this is. The mentalities of the various nations are quite dissimilar. Even among civilised countries there is an enormous difference between people, their customs and their way of life, so it is patently obvious that to mix people who are quite unlike cannot have good results.

I will limit myself to examining the material fundamentals which vary for each nation. The brain of an under-developed person differs from that of a more advanced person. The development of the spirit entity and its expression of will are limited to the possibilities offered it by its physical body.

Great disturbances can result if bodily development has to be derived from such different basic elements.

We will talk about this again in another chapter. For today it suffices that I have drawn attention to the matter. Until now it has rarely been considered in the analysis of mental illnesses and symptoms of neurosis.

The incorrect interpretation of the value of sexual intercourse. Its dangers and necessary clarification.

I LAST spoke about the fact that the physical constitution of people in other parts of the world differs from ours and that inter-marriage of dissimilar races is not advisable and can often be very harmful.

It will be pointed out to me that proof to the contrary exists; children of mixed marriages develop well and have quite normal natures. But it can be argued that hereditary traits are often not apparent in the first generation but rather in the third or fourth. At any rate the utmost caution is advised. The education of youngsters should also include this subject in case the opportunity — not to say the danger — rears its head.

But let us go a step further and consider what people have to do if they have symptoms that are unusual for their race.

According to the medical fraternity these are mental illnesses or illnesses of the nervous system. In point of fact they are not an illness, but a degeneracy for which there is no cure.

Nevertheless it is imperative that an attempt is made to point such a person in the right direction and by feeling one's way into the condition incurred through no fault of his, try to help him to adjust to his prevailing way of life. Contempt, disdain or even exclusion from human society is certainly not indicated; instead there should be helpful understanding, forgiveness, and a thorough instruction at a social, mental and spiritual level. Only good treatment can help remedy such lapses and open the door to a better way of life for him. The fact that he is not responsible for his condition must be the underlying thought. Only endless patience will help.

Now I want to speak of other things which are closely allied to such matters. This is the attitude towards lapses in sexual life.

These are not only found frequently in the relationships I have just mentioned. No, unfortunately they also occur in the civilised world.

People do not pay much attention to the role of affection and antipathy in life. In their opinion their sex life is the necessary basis for a normal existence. A person who avoids the sexual drive and lives on a purely spiritual level is abnormal and deprives himself of the best of what life has to offer.

This is a great mistake and it is fortunate that it is so. People who have no mind for this material form of love are often more advanced than others.

At first glance this seems to be a contradiction. There must be sexual intercourse to ensure the procreation of mankind and make recurring incarnations possible. This brings me to the crux of the matter.

Procreation is the basic purpose of intercourse between two people, but without pure love it is ill-starred.

It is quite wrong that the word "love" is used for intercourse. As I said at the beginning of my messages, people must find new concepts and expressions which clearly convey the difference between sensual desire and all-embracing love. It is the difference of night and day, which is why intercourse is usually followed by bitter disappointment. It is a good sign if a person experiences a vacuum afterwards because everybody has the same reaction if he is honest with himself. If he is dissatisfied with this perfectly normal vacuum, he seeks heightened pleasure and diversion. But this only leads to ever-increasing dissatisfaction because contentment will never be found in this direction. Only very few people are clever enough to realise that sexual pleasure never contributes to happiness or progress.

Some seek to lay the shortcoming on their partners or they blame themselves for what they consider to be an inexcusable deficiency. Such people suffer more than others because they don't dare to discuss the matter or to entrust themselves to a doctor or a third person.

It is a subject which requires careful consideration. Youngsters growing to adulthood should be thoroughly instructed in its various aspects.

Just give them an indication of what I write about and you will see what bitter disappointment will be spared many a struggling and searching young person. They are problems one can discuss. Thank God the times are past when it was impossible to talk about love and marriage and attendant matters in the family circle. How many youngsters have, through faulty education, landed in bad company and circles that took advantage of their ignorance and twisted their minds.

It is a very important part of their education. They must be guided to observe an equilibrium and not expect heaven on earth. A vacuum, aversion, disappointment and quarrels will instead be the order of the day if true love - a willingness to sacrifice and renounce one's own interests - is not the basis of a union. Where this is lacking and the greatest happiness is expected only from sexual intercourse the result will be physical, emotional, and mental suffering.

Physical suffering is a sign of overstrain on the organs, of activity beyond the generally known limits imposed by nature.

A sense of shame and fear of punishment prevents the person concerned from seeking out a doctor in good time.

This is why, particularly with sexual illnesses, it is so difficult for doctors to take early action. Many of these cases could have been nipped in the bud if the education of youngsters had dealt with these matters.

Instead the younger generation is generally left to drift or storm into adulthood. The older generation is then scandalised to discover that it has gone astray and to all intents and purposes is more depraved and rotten than its own.

People must realise that the faulty development of their offspring will be their burden and should give serious attention to remedial instruction. Not when the disaster has occurred but as a preventative measure, based on their own experiences. This requires the courage to admit what they had wrongly expected of life; where disappointment instead of pure joy, certainty and peace had to be suffered because they had not been introduced to the correct interpretation of life.

Do not, therefore, use "love" for a behaviour that seldom has any connection with the word. Prove that you can pass it by. It cannot last and satisfy you forever.

So much has already been said and written about this. The great mistake is that sex is considered the normal basis for sharing a life and aversion to it a sign of illness or deficiency.

Medical science must free itself from this point of view because it has no way of knowing in how far spiritual maturity calls for denial. If it is a matter of a purely physical defect like underdeveloped organs, then this will account for the negative attitude. But it does not mean that these organs are the cause. On the contrary, organs can atrophy or be insufficiently developed because in the spiritual basis of the blueprint brought to earth such a denial has already been established. One must be extremely careful of a diagnosis and take into account that it is quite unimportant whether a person does or does not show an inclination for sex. A healthy and normal way of life does not make this requirement.

Let this be an indication to individual psychologists that in evaluating a person's life it is not important whether a person makes a satisfactory marriage partner or is not at all interested in marriage.

Community consciousness is the highest aspiration to aim for. It leads to a happy life.

The effects of abnormal unions and methods of healing the resultant degeneracies. The other-worldly point of view on the termination of pregnancies.

WHAT I have told you about not mixing races and people at different stages of development is very important, but more important is how to react when dealing with the offspring of such couples.

As I have said, it is mainly physical divergence which causes abnormal development. It is the effect on the spirit entity along with other conditions which prevents natural growth. Let us examine a particular group of these people, namely a group in which the underdeveloped organism has the upper hand. We will soon notice that their habits and goals in life have nothing in common with those of more advanced persons.

Medical science defines this condition as "a character deficiency" or as "acquired tendencies," perhaps also "a disposition inherited from parents." But it has not occurred to any scientist that the development is according to set principles and could not be otherwise. So in cases where the alien predisposition dominates, an adaption to the more highly developed civilised form will very seldom be possible.

In such cases the only solution is surveillance by good doctors, constant tests to maintain the sexual organs in a healthy condition and the education of youngsters to correct behaviour towards these surely very pitiful people. If it is no longer possible to re-educate them towards what for us are normal living conditions, then those who could be harmed by them must be correctly informed and warned not to have sexual contact. In this way much suffering and damage could be avoided.

Every psychiatrist knows how many major illnesses, even though they are only organic, can result from such unhealthy and abnormal unions.

I mention only organic suffering because the spirit entity as such cannot be destroyed. Only the organic brain becomes sick and is unable to perform its duty so that the soul is handicapped and over-taxed and cannot carry out the spirit entity's instructions. As I see it, this is a time waster, an obstruction to emotional and spiritual progress. This condition will continue until the sickly and unnatural behaviour has been eliminated and the organs can resume their normal functions. Great care must go into the treatment of such people. Their attitude to life must be correctly orientated. In fact, this is the most essential pre-requisite for a cure.

It is quite wrong to try and heal them with drugs and radical treatment. The only result will be indifference to human sentiments and there will never be an improvement, nor will any spiritual development be achieved. These pitiful creatures are also human and belong to the community. This is why they require the utmost attention. A doctor does not have the right to disturb and impede the natural functions necessary to maintain life. Every person must find the correct path on his own. To do so, he will need careful education. These are not creatures of a secondary category. They are human beings who seek progress or must be stimulated to do so.

All human life deserves the same respect and consideration. Arrogance towards others has no place in a correct philosophy of life even though a person may consider himself lucky enough to have reached a higher stage of development and has recognised his desire to progress. This is why he must include contact with less developed people in his programme for life and be convinced that his task also includes dealing correctly with them: that he must not destroy but lend a helping hand. It is certainly a tedious undertaking which requires great empathy. It can be learned even if, at first, the mentality of the patient cannot be established. In the beginning many a mistake will be made before insight is gained and experience enables norms and rules to be established.

This work must always be undertaken with love and the firm resolution to serve humanity. It is not a case of the stronger fighting the weaker without consideration for the outcome.

It is important whether a doctor dominates or serves his patients. He may only dominate if his power is governed by good intentions and love.

While on this theme I must also say a word about the termination of a pregnancy or the "killing" of an unborn child.

Strictly speaking it is an operation on matter alone which does not affect the spirit and soul. One should not talk of killing because the earthly meaning of this word is the flight or separation of the spirit entity from the material body.

Incarnation only occurs in the last stages of birth. The termination of a pregnancy in its early stages can therefore only be compared to an organic operation.

This is the material point of view, but the spiritual point of view, which takes into consideration the development according to set principles which every person must follow, is different.

Earlier generations considered having a child born out of wedlock sinful because civilisation and the Church condemned it.

But it is a matter for medical consideration whether the birth of a child is desirable and advisable; it is not a social matter.

Only a doctor can and dare decide whether the physical condition of a woman bearing a child allows for its healthy development. Only in the most extreme cases should he agree to a preventative operation. Such a decision should have nothing to do with social factors or the egotistical wishes of the parents.

If a woman falls pregnant intentionally or by mistake, it is only right that she goes the whole way and takes on the tasks which she or her fate has decreed and carries them out to the best of her ability.

How often the greatest despair preceding a birth turns to the greatest happiness and the most wonderful life task for a mother who went her own way unswervingly.

Here the doctor, especially in his function as a good psychologist, has his most rewarding task.

I have introduced this subject here because it plays an important role in the choice of a partner for intercourse. A birth may not be prevented because it is the result of a coupling of unequally developed partners. It is the association that must be avoided in the first place. I want to draw attention to this and stress that once a step has been taken along this road it cannot and may not be retraced. Furthermore, it is not possible at the outset to determine whether the disposition of the more advanced parent will prevail in the child's physical development, ensuring that it is both normal and healthy according to our standards.

These are matters which an earthly doctor cannot decide or clarify. Incarnation occurs in accordance with rules and regulations that a human being will find strange and inscrutable. In this regard it is only possible for him to heed healthy, material fundamentals and try to eliminate disruptive influences.

This chapter raises several subjects requiring careful consideration. We will learn more about them in the course of time.

Of fundamental importance is the viewpoint that the termination of a pregnancy is to be considered an operation on a mother's body and not the killing of a human being. In this context please bear in mind the question of the justification for such an operation. It can have repercussions on the spirit entity's future development without necessarily being the serious crime it is today according to existing legal opinion and the opinion of society.

It is quite in order to apply strict regulations and to insist on extremely careful examinations. However, the consequences do not affect the community, but only the person who makes use of forbidden possibilities for egotistical reasons.

Inherited degeneracies. Epilepsy, multiple sclerosis and their causes.

OUR topic today has not yet been mentioned in my messages. It is the subject of inherited degeneracies, which differ from those resulting from outside influences attracted in the course of a lifetime.

I want to begin with an illness which has already occurred in parents and could not be cured through appropriate treatment, an operation or because the patient, in his negligent approach to life, never consulted a specialist.

It is brought on by physical deficiencies and either underdeveloped or badly developed organs, particularly the brain.

One of the main illnesses of this kind is epilepsy. Every neurologist and psychiatrist is familiar with its symptoms which in every case are more or less alike. The attacks associated with this complaint are quite unforeseen and occur without visible or tangible reason. They cannot be contained if a doctor is not called in at the time. As the patient can move and function more or less freely afterwards, he tends not to call for medical care. Only where friends or family have to suffer the convulsions and stand by helplessly is it to be expected that the patient will receive the relevant treatment.

In the main he can be cured if he receives medical attention in the early stages. Then there is no longer any danger for normal, healthy procreation.

But very often such illnesses occur in a child's early years. In this case it is undoubtedly a throwback to the parents who are wholly responsible for the degeneracy.

This brings me to the problem of prevention and responsibility, a subject that is largely neglected and one that should be given considerable attention in an adolescent's educational programme.

The time will probably come when science will accord more attention than it does today to the timely prevention of illnesses and degeneracies. It is not sufficient to issue a warning after a doctor has been advised of the condition purely by chance. There must be an obligation for constant controls to be created such as are the norm for infectious diseases.

Epilepsy particularly is an illness that is far more widespread than one supposes. Medical science knows this, but is reluctant to introduce radical measures to combat its continual spread because the cause is not fully known.

I will name it. It is a grave disturbance of the circulation caused by the degeneration of that part of the brain which guides and actuates regular breathing and, consequently, regular circulation.

In its early stages, which means if the patient has only suffered attacks for a short while, a total cure is possible if the affected sections of the brain are suitably treated or at least strengthened so they can perform their duties.

Strengthening can be done through beaming the brain with electricity but only in very small, careful doses which do not produce a state of shock, otherwise the opposite effect could result. The weakened sections of the brain would not withstand the sudden stimulation and be paralysed.

Considerable experience has been gathered for medical treatment, but I will not discuss it here.

Incurable cases, or those which improve after treatment but then suffer a relapse, can only be kept in a controlled state.

I have chosen this degeneracy because it illustrates most clearly how important it is to take timely precautionary measures so that people who have it are taught not to have children.

There is also a second reason. It is an illness that is always inherited. Not only is it transferred from one generation to the next, but it becomes stronger. This heritage is a prime example of the sins of the fathers caused by the union of two people who are not equally developed and have not paid sufficient attention to their choice of partners.

Multiple sclerosis has not been greatly researched. It is a dreadful disease which ravages and erodes the body.

Unlike epilepsy, it is not necessarily inherited; it is an infection similar to cancer. Both are the bane of humanity as tuberculosis once was and will continue to be so until a cure is found for them. I am not permitted to say what it will be, but I can offer the consolation that it will soon be possible to fight these serious organic conditions and at least lessen their dreadful effects.

That mutiple sclerosis is a purely organic illness is shown by the fact that mental activity can be maintained and indeed increased as long as the relative nerve centres and brain sections have not been affected. Paralysis of the limbs is not caused by a defective brain function but is due to the dying off of the peripheral nerves in the damaged spinal cord.

This is why it is foolish to include this illness in the category of mental diseases. It has probably been done because it was assumed that it was a matter of psychic degeneracy or an abnormal way of life. How much damage has been done to the poor people afflicted with this illness. Quite wrongly they were, and still are, treated like lepers. Medical science has not yet discovered preventative measures for this form of suffering.

Unlike epilepsy, this disease cannot be passed on as long as a person has no symptoms of the illness. But should a woman with this disease conceive or fall pregnant by a man who has it, the pregnancy should be terminated immediately. I have chosen this example to illustrate the justification for such action. It is equally so in the case of epilepsy because the illness is aggravated in offspring.

People contemplating marriage should be forced to undertake thorough check-ups as long as such examinations are not standard procedure.

Having a family is not always life's most desirable goal. Everybody can progress to fulfil his blueprint and prove his worth in other ways.

People afflicted with organic defects and hereditary diseases should consider these as warning signs that they have been earmarked to go through life and master their tasks alone. In this way they will realise sooner and more easily where they have to seek their assignments.

Once they recognise the reason for their affliction, women can use their motherly gifts everywhere. And no suffering is so great that the possibility of fulfilling a useful occupation which inspires self-confidence and security cannot be undertaken.

Of course, I speak only of those hereditary diseases that do not affect the mental and emotional aspects. As I have already mentioned, only physical, therefore purely material qualities, are hereditary. So-called mental illnesses are brain impediments in so far as they affect the ability to think.

The hereditary transmission of so-called mental illnesses is also to be traced back to organic changes. As I have already explained, the effect is stronger in children than in their forbears.

It is a very serious problem and one that cannot be understood and explained through general tenets. Every case must be individually examined, and the origin and intensity established.

But whenever there are signs that the normal development of a child could be in jeopardy, a pregnancy should be avoided.

Renunciation is never a mistake, but the unfounded and medically unjustified termination of a pregnancy is.

We will have more to say about this subject in order to have a complete picture of the requirements for a healthy life of the parents in order to produce healthy offspring.

MESSAGES FROM A DOCTOR IN THE FOURTH DIMENSION

A doctor's opinion of human modes of behaviour based on general norms in relation to individual personality.

TODAY I will deal with a different subject which I have already mentioned but not enlarged upon. It is this: to what extent should a doctor consider the behaviour of the individual in relation to basic norms and make them equally applicable to everybody? To what extent is he compelled to examine the individual's emotions and mode of behaviour in relation to his overall personality?

It is a subject that requires a great deal of leeway and sympathetic understanding: an ability to rise above the crowd and examine matters objectively.

Every individual is unique. His emotions and philosophy of life cannot be compared with those of anybody else. This I have indicated in an earlier chapter.

But there are reactions that are, or should be, the same for everybody.

These are external stimuli which affect the soul and trigger a universal reaction. They follow a set pattern, although the degree of intensity may not be the same. For example, every person has the same bodily reaction to a sharp blow. We have known this for a long time and base our physical examinations on this knowledge.

What is not so clearly known is the emotional effect. Every soul reacts differently to a stimulus, even an external one. A blow can trigger various responses. It can have a shock effect; it can be considered hurtful — by this I mean offensive — or considered hostile. The influence just depends on the individual character of the person concerned.

What I am saying is that it is impossible always to have the same response to a stimulus. But it is just this difference that gives us the opportunity to study the various capacities for being effected, determine the degree of mental and emotional maturity, locate blockages affecting the mind and the sensibilities and find a treatment that is able to produce a more or less harmonious adjustment between the intellect and feelings of each individual.

This opens up a whole new field, one I will discuss again later on.

But how should we approach the most significant fundamental

problems caused by these countertendencies? Primarily with open eyes and without prejudice.

For an abnormal attitude or a shortcoming in one person can be accepted or allowed in another without criticism; the general behaviour must just coalesce in a harmonious pattern. Probably nobody has, as yet, achieved this state. This is precisely the reason that we always wish to return to earth and must do so, because we wish to progress to the highest state of perfection.

Now I want to deal with some concrete issues. We have to differentiate between modes of behaviour that are due to the physique and those caused by the spirit which are in accordance with the degree of maturity it has attained. In the material sense these are physical characteristics and influence the soul.

A healthily developed person who conforms to an accepted standard should not have physical inhibitions. This is the first norm we should take for granted.

Shyness and disturbed feelings of guilt, incompetence, indecency or blameworthiness in exaggerated measure are the results of physical weaknesses and an abnormal development. In so far as they equate with the degree of degeneracy they are quite natural and form an integral part of the individual's personality, even though it is to be regarded as a hindrance to his development. In all probability it will not be possible for him to overcome this quite natural attitude. It would be wrong to interpret it as anomalous.

It is a different matter with people who are normal and healthy, but nevertheless show signs of an inferiority complex because they are convinced they do not conform to the generally accepted norms. They are emotionally oppressed and run the risk of disturbing, or even destroying, their health through this incorrect attitude.

We are familiar with the results of wrong thinking in this field in every degree of intensity. They have to be treated at various levels, and not necessarily by a neurologist or psychiatrist. Parents and teachers are the first to notice these sentiments. From early childhood, they are duty bound to encourage self-confidence, physical security and normal development. People who have been guided and cared for in this respect will be less inclined to succumb to exaggerated reactions. A person who feels inferior in whatever way looks for compensation whilst physical inferiority often leads to exaggerated physical actions. As in all things, the happy medium has to be sought and the growing child's vision has to be pointed towards it. In this way mistakes — even crimes — that would have occurred in the future can be guarded against.

People who suffer from a physical handicap, who are, for example, crippled from birth, must be very carefully and lovingly examined and guided. Not everybody afflicted in this manner suffers on account of it, but a person has seldom achieved such a degree of spiritual maturity that, in spite of comparing himself with his normally developed and healthy fellow-men, he takes his own shortcomings for granted and seeks to make his way in a field where physical handicaps are not important. In the main these people suffer visibly.

Those who show indifference suffer the most emotionally. Obviously there can be no infallible indication of this attitude. Only very tender insight into the psyche of such people allows the doctor to diagnose it.

Let us not be deterred from helping those who are not an open book. Their reserve should incite us - I mean we doctors who explore the human psyche and soul - to dig deep into the secrets of every single one of them to get a clear picture of their life. This should not be done to enrich our knowledge but rather to heal and liberate them from oppressive ideas.

I have already mentioned that a patient seldom tells the truth. This observation should not be incorrectly interpreted. It does not mean that a patient always lies to his doctor. No, he doesn't know himself: his erroneous concept of life causes him to see things incorrectly. It is indeed his opinion, but he is either mistaken or determined not to let the truth well up from his innermost being. Very often he tries to show himself in a good light to his doctor, to make a good impression to — as he thinks — win his favour and be highly esteemed. Relatively seldom does he bare his most private feelings without reserve of his own accord.

This would be an ideal basis for the doctor to proceed from, but he must check if the patient's information is not exaggerated in the negative sense and paints a far blacker picture than he deserves. It is a task which above all requires the doctor's thorough knowledge and objectivity as well as the faculty to see things from a higher point of view in order to be able to make a correct assessment of the patient's pattern of behaviour.

Now I will discuss how to deal with such problems. Assuming

that the doctor is a highly developed person, he will let the patient talk freely. He will study his way of life, his attraction to or dislike of various mental activities and then try to recognise in which spheres the patient has considerable or particular abilities. This will be the starting point for effective treatment. The patient will be happy to realise that valuable emotions are stirring his soul. Automatically, his oppressive thoughts related to his physical defects will be deflected.

The doctor must not stop here. He must not only consider the physical fundamentals on which he has based his treatment. In order to stimulate the patient's correct attitude to life, he should encourage him to make use of his talents to the benefit of his fellow-men.

Of course, I do not talk here of people who are severely handicapped mentally, but rather, I would say, of the cross-section of mankind which is not yet in a position to find the right path on its own and for whose mental progress much must be done so that conversely physical inferiority disappears progressively as a result.

Mental maturity ensures healthy foundations for physical heredity. This in turn provides the necessary basis for progressive and uninhibited mental development.

Reactions and their importance in a medical examination and the establishment of a perfect diagnosis

YESTERDAY I spoke of the fact that man, considered as an individual, is unique and his reaction to impressions is in accordance with his spiritual maturity. Therefore, it is not easy for doctors to define these reactions and always make an immediate and correct diagnosis; particularly as everybody receives and makes use of impressions according to his personality and blueprint for life.

Now I want to examine which reactions are generally considered normal and what the doctor has — and has not — to do if unnatural reactions are observed. In the physical sphere the human body reacts mainly to heat and cold. Both have average tolerance values. But in addition there are other values which indicate certain disturbances. By this I mean to say that all people do not experience heat and cold in the same way and endure them without damage to their system.

MESSAGES FROM A DOCTOR IN THE FOURTH DIMENSION

If in my practice, for example, I established that a person could generally tolerate exposure to sudden cold, but his general state of health was disturbed afterwards, this was an indication that a somewhat abnormal reaction was present and the ability to produce the necessary adjustment was lacking.

In normal circumstances a person exposed to conditions of cold — which naturally should not last too long — generates warmth through his own circulation to restore the necessary balance. A weak or weakened circulation is not able to restore this balance: the cold does not stimulate but further weakens the circulation and creates a disturbance which affects the soul via the nervous system.

Short treatments with cold applied with care are often of great value. They stimulate the organism and have a balancing and calming effect afterwards. Not so with people who are weak and whose circulation is not in order.

This is a small example of the many different reactions which are well-known to medical science. Treatments have shown good results and are widely used in naturopathy.

They are a valuable section of the various forms of treatment and show how, in actual fact, natural powers should be used much more than chemical remedies. The latter probably combat a particular illness effectively, but the side effects and damaging consequences in other areas and on other organs are not known and occasionally are very dangerous. But this is by the way.

Our topic is reactions, their importance in medical examinations and the establishment of correct diagnoses.

So a person who reacts abnormally to the cold treatment should be examined more carefully. There are various reasons for this reaction. It is possible that in his youth - for such treatment is usually directed at an older person - the patient was pampered and spoiled. He may have been subjected to more warmth than was necessary and lived an unhealthy life so that the cold treatment will now be a shock to his system. In such a case normal physical care has to be applied slowly and carefully to avoid a reaction of power loss and a consequent emotional drain. But if a person enjoyed normal bodily care in his youth, if he was a sporty type and there was no evidence of coddling, then the abnormal reaction must have other reasons. These must be found.

Apart from organic ills which can be mechanically established, the doctor will generally find that psychic influences are all-important. They are to be found in an unnatural way of life, an incorrect philosophy of life, in emotional stress brought on by demanding or one-sided work and so on. It is a huge field that unfolds here and awaits treatment and elimination in so far as this is possible within the confines of civilisation. Man is purely and simply nervous. He is weakened; he is spent. These are the key indications of symptoms that have such disastrous influences that it is worth finding ways to combat them by all possible means. One must only begin to establish the causes correctly so that the help extended to the individual can be magnified and all mankind enjoys lasting benefit.

There are as many varieties of emotional disturbances as there are people. The causes are often the same or similar, but the effects are so vastly different that blanket treatment cannot be applied.

But one rule serves everybody. Take care! The soul is a delicate instrument; its chords have to be handled with extreme caution if they are not to be put out of tune or perhaps even torn apart.

Every doctor should write this sentence on the first page of his diary in capital letters. He must always bear in mind that he is face to face with a precious immortal being who is, more than he knows and will ever realise, subject to his power and domination. This is why he should work not just to carry out the dictates of his profession in a mechanical fashion, but to progress to the highest calling. This will afford him the correct power and ability to feel and investigate the sorrows and ailments and the negative influences of the people entrusted to him.

I must keep repeating that every illness is seated in the soul, and that it does not sufffice to heal or remove an organ without paying the greatest attention to the patient's frame of mind and life.

Apart from mechanical influences, which in the case of abnormal reactions lead to the conclusion that the soul is either burdened or obstructed, there are of course those which are caused directly by the spirit entity or by an incorrect attitude to life and its purpose. This can be traced back to the fact that the spirit entity has not yet understood the true fundamentals of human existence and must change its views in order to move onto the right track. In such cases there are no negative organic reactions but rather a lack of desire to recognise the natural sources that would heighten the vital energy and so the good effect is suppressed and rejected. A favourable and beneficial effect can only be expected when the patient switches to the correct outlook and helps by working in his own mental field.

Every doctor knows how much he needs the co-operation of the patient in the case of physical and, often too, mental illnesses. He can point the way, but the patient must follow it. One of the doctor's main duties is to convince him of the importance and truth of this tenet.

We have drawn up a list of fundamental modes of behaviour for a doctor. It is increasingly obvious in which fields he can dominate his patient and when, on the other hand, he must allow his intuitive faculties free reign in order to recognise and correctly assess the patient's individuality, his personality.

I suppose I tend to say the same things over and over again, but I am forced to do so in order to combine these words in all possible contexts and constantly draw attention to them as everything must be built on them; as everything can only be built on them.

The influences of the spirit entity which contradict Nature's universally valid rules must be carefully examined. It must be considered whether they are in accordance with the patient's life. In such cases it is necessary to be extremely careful not to disturb the course of life, not to make the individual uncertain and bring him into a condition of conflict.

It is not necessary to respect the way of life of every individual to the point of regarding it as unchangeable. No, once the personality and its life course have been identified the great task of transformation begins; it should point to higher goals. We are going to spend some time on this subject and bring to paper many thoughts - even those that are taken for granted - that are worth discussing and should be adopted by doctors and medical science and given more attention than they have received until now.

Repercussions of emotional impressions.
Common sense.

YESTERDAY I spoke about influences affecting the organism and the resulting conclusions.

Now I want to examine other powers that are much more difficult to determine and whose effects cannot be so easily defined and recognised.

These are purely emotional impressions evoked by thoughts, words and events that have been witnessed and read about. We have to begin with the earliest years of childhood as a child's impressions are particularly far-reaching in both the good and bad sense.

A child who is protected from noise and an ugly environment, who grows up in sunshine and good air and is cared for lovingly, has the best basis in later years to choose that which will benefit its progress. Such a person will be able to judge instinctively if what happens to him is in accordance with the experiences he has already undergone and will, of his own accord, reject whatever is in conflict with it. These will not only be external impressions, but all influences that do not conform to the fundamentals he has accepted.

A child who stumbles forward into life in an ugly, noisy environment without love and kindness and is not guided with consideration can only fall back on the blueprint it has brought to earth. At first it will consider the given conditions the correct ones and will follow the direction offered by its surroundings. Sooner or later, according to its degree of spiritual maturity, it will realise that this set of circumstances is not ideal and will forge a new path — its own. But sometimes this realisation never dawns.

The basics now offer a wide variety of directions. A normal, healthy youngster who receives the best care for the furthering, development and fulfilment of its blueprint can expect a happy, carefree, positive childhood. It is easy to imagine how many ways of development there must be if the progress and maturity of the personality is based only on ideal fundamentals. From this a conclusion can be drawn if the opposite occurs and what has to be taken into consideration if the conditions are negative.

I have already stated that reincarnation follows a set pattern based on eternal, irrevocable laws, so that it must not be considered unjust if the material fundamentals are so dissimilar. But this does not mean that matters must be left to run their course and you have to resign yourself to the fact that all characters are different and happiness is unevenly distributed in the world. Man's knowledge is restricted to a limited horizon which does not permit him a clear view of his entire evolution. He is forced to choose the right path through free will, to err until he finds truth and his progress is assured.

Wise people know that only the search for truth leads to happiness. It is their vocation to help their fellow men in their endeavours. In so doing, they will develop further and expedite their progress in the best possible way.

But let us return to the subject of emotional impressions and their effects.

I have already stated that man is not inclined and willing to reveal his deep, innermost secrets. It requires total confidence in his doctor, parents or teacher.

If a person is confronted with circumstances or events which were unfamiliar to him before, he tries to explain them to himself, determine whether they are positive, beneficial or without consequence, and decide how to incorporate them into his philosophy of life.

In emotional matters personal judgement cannot always assess a situation so the soul only accepts the impression without forming a concrete opinion. Once the impression has been absorbed the soul reacts instinctively, either with approval or aversion.

A doctor often hears his patient say, "I heard (or saw) these dreadful things, but thought no more about them." But aversion was apparent. Here lies the danger for the soul. It receives impressions, but either because of a lack of free will or on account of weakness does not transmit them to the spirit entity. The worry remains because the explanation which would clear up the matter is lacking.

However stressful and oppressive an impression, an explanation can unburden the soul. Reason prevails over sentiment and weakens its effect. But a necessary condition is a healthy intelligence and a clear insight into happenings in the material world and their purpose.

For example, I have already pointed out that the death of a beloved person would not cause such heart-rending grief if people would learn to appreciate why they have to suffer and renounce relationships. This is probably the most drastic example I can give, but it occurs so frequently in daily life that it would not be difficult to apply the same common sense to lesser occurrences and dismiss them within minutes.

Now, for the first time we have used the words "common sense" and we are going to study them in relation to the soul and the spirit.

The generally accepted meaning of common sense is the avoidance or renunciation of whatever is unsuitable or fulfils tasks which instinctively you would prefer to avoid but for some reason seem to be necessary.

It necessitates a switching-off of feeling, or alternatively, pushing it into the background and replacing it with what is purely mental reflection.

You may not speak of common sense when something is undertaken reluctantly, when in point of fact the opposite course of action is instinctively desired. This is not common sense: it is submission due to compulsion and command. There is a big difference between the two. It must be made clear.

A child is often considered sensible because it does everything its parents or teacher consider correct. If the child considers it correct, then you may justifiably call it sensible. But it could equally well have acted out of convenience, laziness in working out the matter for itself or fear of punishment and contempt.

A child's own will is normally so strong that it is almost impossible to persuade it to accept another opinion without opposition.

Many parents are of the opinion that their children should love them and be obedient and accept their views without resistance out of veneration or in recognition of the fact that they are older and speak from experience. We already know how wrong this is and that it is a totally erroneous concept of education to force a personal opinion and personal experiences onto a young person.

Common sense always implies a clear-cut personal decision and logical reasoning that only this and no other solution is possible and correct for the matter in question. It is also moderation personified, a hint of the equilibrium which is so desirable for us in every possible context. Gradually we see how harmonious thought and feeling should be constituted and how it must be directed if we wish to raise children to become mentally and emotionally balanced adults.

Common sense can no more be forced upon a person than can charity. It must be exemplified and put to the test in every situation in life.

Very few people can do this, although everybody can observe and criticise himself. It is very difficult to make an honest personal assessment. Either you seek an excuse or exaggerate and instead of reasonable judgement there is condemnation, which in some cases can be very dangerous.

In all his actions man must endeavour to deliberate clearly. He must not allow himself to be impelled senselessly by the feeling that everything is controlled by fate. This is contrary to free will.

Deliberation means to react mentally, not emotionally, to come to a logical decision without sensitive influence. This is not easy. Therefore, education and guidance is necessary.

We will close for today and continue tomorrow with the transition from common sense to knowledge and truth and their effect on the soul and spirit. It is a pleasant subject and worth discussing in all its variations.

Correct deliberation the way to knowledge and wisdom. Memory, the basis for the spirit entity's activity. Imagination, the mirror image of past existence in the world beyond.

YESTERDAY we spoke about common sense and deliberation as opposed to compulsion and submission to foreign will.

Today we are going to consider where good and bad deliberation can lead and what real value it has for spiritual progress. Correct deliberation, which is careful consideration and a search for the proper decision, is the way to knowledge and wisdom.

To assimilate a fact without first classifying it within the realm of truth and abiding realities is only a passing awareness. Such an impression seldom produces a lasting concept and is soon forgotten. It is a purely intuitive perception.

People who are able to transfer emotional impressions rapidly to a mental level and have the will to retain them are able to store endless riches in the way of knowledge in their memories.

Knowledge is the main and most important basis for progress in the search for truth. But knowledge, as I have already indicated, is not wisdom and far removed from truth in the divine sense. Knowledge is the first step and does not entitle a person to squandering it. The road must be travelled further; knowledge must be constantly tested as to its value or worthlessness and developed only for the benefit of mankind.

Man is seldom inclined to switch from passive activity - the absorption of facts and of more or less interesting impressions - to active, creative work. This is very often because of laziness, or the mistaken conviction that knowledge alone is the ultimate achievement in the incarnate world. Or perhaps he is hampered by feelings of inferiority; he simply feels he is not capable of such work.

Here again the teacher or doctor must intervene when he sees that the young person or the patient has acquired great knowledge which should be utilised. The precondition is that the doctor is aware of the fact that great knowledge alone makes a person only partially happy and if he fails to make use of it, he will depart from earthly life without having turned it to good account.

Knowledge need not always be erudition. In all spheres of human life there are fields of knowledge to be perfected as the first step towards development. In the fourth dimension the evaluation of mental attainment is quite different to its present scientific appraisal on earth.

A person who knows exactly to which goal the exploitation of acquired knowledge leads, but is not willing to undertake it, commits a great mistake which he will have to make good in a later life.

It is as well to know this and teach it. Many a person has the inclination to accomplish work that brings progress to mankind, but considers himself presumptuous, unauthorised and not called to do this work. In such cases, real efforts must be made so that the powers lying dormant are utilised for the good of the community instead of being suppressed.

I have said that knowledge is only the beginning. I dare say that in the case of more or less healthy and normally developed people there is not one who does not possess abilities that only have to be awakened.

I spoke of memory which absorbs and retains impressions and will now try and explain how people should understand this.

The spirit entity absorbs impressions and appraises and classifies them with the help of the brain. It retains thoughts according to its will and its ability to work within the body. I have already mentioned that if the brain, for instance, is not properly developed, it handicaps the spirit entity. Just as a person cannot move about freely in a very small room, so too the spirit entity cannot in its earthly prison.

The spirit's freedom of movement is greatest in the first years of life as obstructions caused by a sick or disturbed soul do not occur so frequently. This is why experiences of early childhood are often retained to an advanced age. In old age, on the other hand, the handicaps due to changes in their brain and reduced vitality cause impressions to be easily forgotten and only fleetingly transferred to the spirit entity.

A poor memory calls for medical tests and allows the doctor to establish physical and mental development.

However a distinction must be made because by no means does an organic weakness indicate that there is a parallel, incurable mental decline.

With suitable treatment to both the organs and the psyche extensive improvement can be attained so that the spirit entity can do justice to all the requirements of the blueprint it has brought along.

We want to observe what can be deduced from the immense power of memories of childhood. The power of recall, the degree of reminiscence, the number of impressions retained show us the freedom of development and the condition of the environment in which the child developed. The kind of impressions and their emotional utilisation indicate whether it grew up in a loving or indifferent atmosphere.

Of course, it is not easy to re-create a perfect picture from what an adult recounts. Memories are sometimes distorted because it is very tempting to gloss over reports or make them interesting and unusual.

But the time span that leads back to the events that have been retained can be examined. The further back memories go, the more uninhibited the child's development was likely to have been. With people who have absolutely no memory of the formative period of their youth it must in general be assumed that their brain is incompletely developed because emotional impressions are usually absorbed freely at this stage. By this I mean that everybody, according to his constitution, has a memory stretching back to early life. If this is missing, there must also be some physical handicap.

There is a similar pattern to be seen in the development of abilities in early childhood. Astonishing results have been established at various times and in every sense. The more freely a child is allowed to grow up and follow its own inclinations, the sooner it will find the direction which the spirit entity needs to fulfil the blueprint it has brought along.

I cannot say this often enough: let your children mature in quiet, untroubled surroundings. Do not try to curtail their soaring thoughts and imagination because these mental images reveal their blueprint. This is the programme they have brought with them. It is the image of their past life in the world beyond which lies dormant in their soul and spirit.

A healthy imagination that leads to good deeds and is filled with love for both animals and man may be an indication that the child does not need firm guidance. On the other hand, ideas that are confused and opposed to everything around it show that guidance towards good and loving deeds is necessary. Parents and teachers have the duty gradually to divert thoughts towards an altruistic, selfless attitude. It is actually one of the finest duties of adults to guide children seeking the truth instead of condemning and forcing them through abstract preaching.

To exemplify what they have to learn through your own behaviour is not only the best, but the only way.

The prevailing theory about heredity is an obstacle to the establishment of truth.

Yesterday I spoke about knowledge; its value and the obligation to make use of it in a way that benefits other people. Great tasks result from this attitude. People would do well always to bear this in mind and not lessen their endeavours to turn their knowledge to good account.

In the first instance I want to call attention to knowledge in the medical field; research in its as yet unexplored areas and attempts to understand the true correlations.

The exponents of individual psychology are at pains to investigate the human psyche in order to establish the causes of various types of behaviour and make use of the results.

But this work is not very advanced because it ignores the links with the cosmic world and tries to draw all its conclusions solely from conditions of incarnate existence.

To begin with, the prevailing theory about heredity blocks the way to establishing the truth. I have mentioned this quite emphatically on various occasions. What has been achieved through example, environment and education has all been tossed indiscriminately into one pot together with similar experiences from an earlier life and the knowledge gained in it.

It cannot be otherwise if one assumes that man should be able to achieve everything in one single lifespan, when actually his present level of development is the result of many, sometimes countless, journeys across the earth and the school of life. As long as this fact is not unequivocally accepted by medical science, all research into the realm of soul and spirit is patchwork.

Particularly in this field better knowledge of the truth is of vital importance to counter the degeneracies and diseases which are not caused by physical conditions or the environment. Those resulting from physical heredity can often be cured without this knowledge. But many additional energies could be called upon and utilised; they are those beyond the material sphere and are only waiting to be recognised and put to work for the benefit of mankind.

I cannot name or describe them and how they work because they are of another substance, another composition, and cannot be classified in terms of earthly medicine.

All that is needed to succeed is belief in our help and in the truth of the ideas we have expounded.

I do not mean to say that all that medical science has achieved until now is inferior, negligible or ineffective. But in view of the possibilities at its disposal, it is insufficient to serve the progress of mankind, improve its general health and help people on their way to spiritual perfection.

How many great medical men make the mistake of not considering the individual as a whole and instead only take into account the technical aspects of organs; the way they function, the way they synchronise, the way they are inter-dependent. Time and again I must emphasise that this can lead to considerable knowledge of the body. The exploitation of this knowledge can benefit the organism as a whole, but it is half the job if the machine is only cleaned out and a defective organ is removed or replaced by an artificial one.

The value of human life is not to be sought in the physical, but rather in the mental zone, the one that functions without a motor. Of course, as I have stressed several times, attention must be paid to keeping the prison of the soul and spirit suitably cared for. If matter is the main fundamental of material life, it must not be neglected.

Everything that exists has been ordained and provided by Divine Omnipotence. For this reason alone it must be respected and watched over. But to consider matter - divorced from spirit and soul - in its perfect state as the pinnacle of what earthly man can be granted is what I condemn and must continue to do.

My attention will be drawn to the fact that as a result of the high standard of medical knowledge today so many diseases and handicaps have been cured. This was not the case several decades ago. But you have no idea how often repairs to material organs result in mental and emotional disturbances because only the sick organ and not the whole individual receives treatment.

I trust my words have been properly understood and I am not accused of denigrating the great men of medicine. I only ask for more understanding, for more care, for a holistic appraisal of a patient.

Wisdom should be the goal of every great scientist. Wisdom in the sense of knowledge combined with universal love. The basis of universal love is service in devotion, kindness and modesty. These qualities must be the basis for progress from knowledge to wisdom, because only by fulfilling these conditions does the erudite man learn to distinguish and probe what is of value and useful or harmful in the whole field of practical experience.

In relation to medicine this can be explained by a very simple example. From his studies the doctor knows that everybody must eat and drink, that everybody needs sleep, and so on. Disturbances resulting from insufficient food, drink, sleep and rest can be corrected and healed by restoring the balance. But he has to be able to assess very accurately in how far weaknesses have occurred as a result of the deprivations and the medical dosages have to be geared accordingly. This is not to be done by simply prescribing more of the same but only by examining the causes and the length of time the resultant effects were evident.

We know that disregard and ignorance in this respect has caused more damage than can be believed. This is simply because knowledge has been applied abstractly without sympathetic understanding and consideration for the available vital energy as well as the organism's interdependence of mental, emotional and physical functions.

From this very simple example one realises how much more dangerous it can be to interfere with an organ without considering the correlations and the influence of soul and spirit.

Once again I make the point: progress in the medical field as far as establishing the function of the organs and their healing is not to be denied and is certainly very welcome. The drawback lies in recognising what, in the negative sense, can be brought about through abstract, impersonal treatment and healing.

It is not easy to be aware of this without recourse to the spiritual. I as a doctor, while true to my profession and serving mankind, did not know it as I do today when I see quite clearly what results are produced through such a one-sided viewpoint.

Even though it is difficult for a doctor to accept that his spendidly successful operation could have negative implications, he should take into consideration that every illness is caused by a handicapped soul and weakened mental vitality. The great practitioners would soon realise how different their diagnoses would be, how far back the patient's psyche would have to be considered and which primary fundamentals would have to be established so that their organic treatments, their inroads into the human body could yield a true, satisfactory result.

I ask only that consideration be given as to how easily this demand could be met, assuming that one is dealing with doctors who consider their work a vocation and wish to work at this level; people who will serve their patients with love, understanding, forgiveness, kindness and great empathy.

Successful work has already been done in this regard, but those concerned are loners. The majority of their materialistically inclined colleagues do not take them seriously.

Of course, what you cannot see you cannot treat and heal as successfully as that which can be seen or measured by machines. This is the difficulty that you must have the courage to overcome.

Useful and useless knowledge.
The necessity of changing the social order.
The unequal distribution of possessions is justified.

I LAST spoke about the fact that knowledge is not wisdom and not one jot closer to truth if it is only stored in a person's memory and not used for the good of people at large. It must be tested and whatever is considered beneficial must be widely promoted.

This is why it is necessary to establish limits for what is useful or useless and even harmful. People are crammed full of knowledge, but too little differentiation is made between what is, and what is not, of value. Useless knowledge is that which oppresses the soul so that it feels dislike or even aversion. It should not be circulated if mankind is to be brought to a peaceful, progressive life. It is absurd to publicise offensive and criminal happenings and educate people to consider them important and interesting, no matter how revolting they are.

The world needs positive teaching about pleasant subjects which fill the soul with compassion and happiness and stimulate it, however slowly, to emulation. Public declarations have a very powerful educational effect. If they are negative, they place an emotional burden on the soul and the spirit has to take issue with them. A relatively highly developed person would have the strength to assess them correctly and make sensible, accurate deductions. A weak person is not always able to react in this way. Clever people avoid such subjects, nor do they look at pictures, listen to reports or talk about matters which they feel are not interesting, endowed with divine grace and inspiration or do not enrich their spiritual progress.

This brings me to the subject of impressions that are purposely conveyed by the irresponsible. Prompted by an overpowering desire for importance and power, they do everything possible to draw attention to themselves and be talked about. They are often not motivated by bad intentions and a particular goal but rather by ambition. They cannot gauge the damage they do to society, just as in the opposite case good intermediaries and people with a calling cannot imagine the positive effects of their work.

These are the people whose paths must be smoothed. Their living conditions must be arranged and secured so that they can fully commit themselves to service. It must be fairly obvious what I am trying to say.

The social order is in need of change. It must be turned towards what is of value as opposed to what is destructive and unhealthy.

The most desirable goal in life is not the so-called freedom of the individual but rather the knowledge that fellowship is all-important. I must always stress the fact that material success is meaningless if it does not benefit other people.

The top priority therefore is re-education to the correct philosophy of life. In this connection I have already stressed that this does not mean a renunciation of worldly goods but rather a harmonious balance between spiritual and material necessities.

Demands only exist where somebody is of the opinion that he has less worldly goods than the next person; this is based on the assumption that everybody should have an equal amount of possessions. The mere statement that this is not so is insufficient to prove the point because not everybody is so spiritually advanced that he can understand the true correlations and divine laws.

This then is where education must begin. It must be radically instilled, but with kindness and a readiness to help.

It is a fact that many a person could demand more for his material life than he receives because civilisation and the interpretation of the law of individual nations prevents equal distribution. It fosters vexation. All wars and hate on earth can be traced back to this fundamental issue.

But there cannot be total equality in the division of material possessions.

You might wonder what this has to do with my scientific field. It is one of the main causes of so much emotional suffering. Matter is the negative aspect of life and has been selected as the means to ensure spiritual progress through its proper control and use.

The mistake lies in overestimating it. This hampers the spirit and soul and forces them to give battle. Not a battle of life and death, of subjugation or annihilation, but one that is a measure of energies and whose goal is their wise utilisation. Matter will always exist and is as indestructible as the spirit and soul. But whereas matter can be considerably altered, the spirit and soul are handicapped and inhibited.

This may appear to be positive, but in the long run it destroys healthy living conditions for people on earth and causes extremely severe upsets and stress for the soul and spirit.

Therefore it is very important that within the various civilisations people are given guidelines and possibilities are created which allow them to produce, acquire and earn what they need for a healthy life.

By this I mean to say that the measures cannot and must not be levelled, but the fundamentals must be available so that everybody can freely organise his life according to his spiritual and physical abilities.

People must be shown how to attain the right attitude in order to decide what is necessary and useful. They must learn to define the limits of what is healthy and desirable. Where this is not obtainable through tenets and good examples, the degeneration of organic development and the often very obvious deterioration of mental abilities, in other words, the obstruction to spirit and soul, will become obvious. This will be a warning sign to the teacher, the doctor or whoever is responsible for the welfare of such people.

I want to stress that from this conclusion it must be deduced that it is not sufficient to distribute material possessions and give people a period of satisfaction and physical well-being through charity. Their energies must be guided to give them both the possibility and incentive to create a healthy existence and a normal basis for life on their own. It must come about through their own free will without pressure. They must have the feeling that they are members of a community that seeks the right path and tries to establish truth. Help such misled souls to find a correct attitude to life; to renounce whatever they possess beyond a necessary sufficiency and you will see how hearts will respond in confidence and the feeling of true equality.

Equality does not mean the equal distribution of material possessions. It means the equal right to acquire and create, through free will and one's own efforts what the material world has to offer.

It is essential always to search for the primary causes of all degeneracies, whether they occur in a single individual or in groups of people. They are rooted in the injustice done to them against which they fight according to their spiritual maturity.

Those guilty of the injustice are not always their contemporaries. The mistakes were made in the past. Now they must really be done away with.

We want to do this step by step and can be certain to succeed if we dedicate ourselves to this task.

Overestimation of matter is caused by the non-fulfilment of the blueprint brought to earth. Clairvoyance a mediumistic ability.

TODAY I wish to write about how people at an advanced spiritual level wander onto the wrong path and are not able to develop and perfect their already extensive knowledge.

Let us go back to the time of birth and examine the influences that constitute such serious stumbling-blocks along life's way that even the blueprint brought along is deflected from its appointed course. Primarily we must choose and study a life programme whose most distinctive features point in the direction of progress and benefit society at large.

This person is a genuine helper of mankind. He has outgrown egotism and realises that to serve other people leads to universal and therefore also individual success. In the world beyond he recognised all the mistakes he made in his last life on earth and now seeks to return to the material world in order to make use of everything in his new life in the best possible way and live and work in the spirit of progress. His desire to pay little attention to material matters, regarding them only as a means to an end, are firmly established: his intentions are both noble and good. .

In order to be able to be true to his vows and furnish evidence of his good intentions, he is born into an environment that offers him few worldly goods as a basis for his existence. It is unpretentious, but the people in it are content and it suits the way of life granted to him. However, the prevailing material outlook predominates. Great common sense and humilty is needed to adapt to these conditions.

The youngster may receive a good education along with the basic guidelines that prepare him for the path he has chosen to follow. But outside influences intervene and force his good intentions into the background. His free will shows him other goals which are in direct conflict with his original purpose. Matter has the upper hand even though, from time to time, his striving for selfless dedication to other people is apparent in good deeds when he actually renounces material advantages. It is clear that this is a case of the spirit being willing but the flesh being weak. This proverb underlines the victory of matter over spirit.

I have already pointed out that material possessions are given to be used and enjoyed. But to use and enjoy does not mean to amass, to waste both energy and time to maintain and increase them to an extent that the individual is in a position to disregard his fellow men and only pays homage to earthly pleasures and succumbs to them in the end.

People must finally learn that they do not live from matter alone; it should only serve to give bodily comfort. To this end, very little of it is necessary.

We only have to consider nations which are content with a minimum of matter and in the eyes of the civilised world exist in circumstances that are simple to the point of being wretched. On the whole they are healthier and more dynamic than other nations, which exist in a plethora of plenty, but only until they come into contact with the exaggerated achievements of the so-called civilised world. This is the reason why the best and spiritually most advanced people in the civilised world mostly come from a very modest background. Here social institutions have already made great efforts to abolish the privileges of the propertied classes.

Individual psychology should pay more attention to these trains of thought. It should not encourage and incite free will to seek material success and recognise proficiency only in the more than average mastery of professional tasks.

The truth is that a person is proficient when in addition to maintaining his existence, which often has little in common with spiritual progress, he attends to his personal development by occupying himself with art, literature and the humanities in order to improve his mental abilities and create a platform for a future vocation.

Here, too, I must stress that my aim is to show people how important it is to have the correct attitude to life. Explain the purpose of this incarnation to them; instill the hope and confidence that every step taken along the right path, no matter how small, means progress and forms an everlasting basis for later existences.

I was telling you about the advanced person who, contrary to his intentions, was led astray from the path he had originally chosen. Once again he will see the error of his ways and strengthen his will. A mistake halts progress, but does not regress it. Despite his placing too much importance on matter, his works for other people were accompanied by good intentions and were successful. But his own progress was hampered, truth was pushed into the background and the help he offered was not in accordance with the possibilities provided for him.

In every situation in life there are parallels both in the spiritual and material spheres, as indeed a set pattern is followed everywhere. The desired result is only brought about by exerting all your energies. The moment our spiritual knowledge is ended by incarnation and hampered by matter we are exposed to material temptation. But this does not apply to everybody. Some people maintain a glimmer of the spiritual realm.

This is why clairvoyants usually came from a background of modest material means. I say "came" because these days the pressure of matter is such that with the striving to acquire it and the immense restlessness it engenders in and around people, all emotional impulses are impaired and the ability for clairvoyance more or less lost.

Only a correct assessment of matter, its moderate use and its subordination to the spiritual sphere will once again bring these abilities to light.

Clairvoyance is a mediumistic power. It is a grace and as such should be used to serve the community in the battle against injustice and crimes committed in earthly life. Just as there are good and bad mediums, so there are honest and dishonest clairvoyants. This results in both the concept and the people blessed with this power to be viewed negatively. As I have already mentioned, abilities based in a spiritual plane and which draw their power from spiritual sources should never be brought into contact with material gain or used to acquire such gain. They will suffer because matter is a negative component which weakens or hampers positive spiritual achievement.

Clairvoyance is quite simply the ability to place oneself on a higher plane, one outside matter and therefore outside the bodily prison, and experience things with spiritual eyes, absorb them into the soul and transmit them to the spirit. One can readily understand that a clairvoyant cannot move indefinitely in other-worldly spheres. To do so requires a conscious attitude, a deliberate passiveness of the soul. Some people are only clairvoyant in dreams and experience prophetic visions and revelations because they have either lost or severely damaged the power to attain total passiveness.

Prophetic dreams, visions, experiencing happenings which

subconsciously and unknowingly occur far away, all these abilities, which according to human opinion are abnormal, belong to the mediumistic sphere even though such encounters are not necessarily intended to be passed on to the public. Nor need they be of general benefit.

A good medium, called to accept communications from the discarnate world, may only use his abilities for the progress of mankind.

Today we can see how the concepts flow into one another and that it is immaterial from which point of view we study them. We will always come back to the fact that matter is subordinate to the spiritual sphere and the correct philosophy of life is all-important.

We will revert to these trains of thought more often and spend as much time as is needed with them until all the correlations have been understood and the way to a correct attitude to life has been quite clearly defined.

The philosophy of life of the individual in relation to the community. The interrelationship of spirit and soul.

IN my writings to date we have heard a lot about life's problems, about ways and means to face them and deal with tasks that often seem insoluble.

Let us summarise these to serve as a preliminary to new trains of thought and reasoning.

We examined the interrelationship between soul, spirit and body as the basis for all further deliberation and briefly indicated what their values and tasks should be: how a healthy soul should be cared for and a handicapped one treated; what, in broad outline, were the causes of degeneracy or rather what caused the spirit to be hampered in its development and which paths mankind should follow for a more rapid evolution in order to ensure a better, more perfect way of life.

However, it is apparent that until now I have not suggested treatments in the various areas I have discussed.

A great many questions occur to people who read my writings. Everyone thinks that problems other than the ones mentioned should be dealt with and seeks explanations in matters that affect his person or have prime significance in his life and career. I must ask you to be patient and believe me when I assure you that in the course of time I will discuss all matters of consequence.

But the ultimate goal remains unchanged — a healthy and positive attitude to life and a striving for knowledge and truth, which for us here in the world beyond must also be the noblest task and the most rewarding aspiration.

As we have already realised, all of us are still at the very beginning of the path and need the help of higher and more advanced spirit entities to maintain progress and enhance our maturity.

I am fully aware of the fact that I do not belong to these great spirits and am not too far above the current human generation. Guided by far more advanced entities, I am allowed to teach what I have been able to learn in the world beyond after a relatively correct earthly existence and to explain the correlations which I have already recognised thanks to my modest spiritual maturity. This will give mankind new ideas and more precise knowledge.

Now I want to pass on to queries which may have arisen in the course of reading the first two volumes.

The individual's outlook on life in relation to his fellow men is the first area I want to consider.

I have already stressed the fact that everybody should have his own philosophy of life which is sufficient unto himself; that his own world has quite definite boundaries so that his personal outlook cannot apply to the next person. But the fundamental interpretations of the purpose of life must be made available to everyone, for he must not consider he can do, think and feel exactly as he pleases, without having to account both to himself and to those around him for his actions.

These fundamentals can be sub-divided under various headings. There are those which concern the soul, the spirit, and the body with its functions and those that not only relate to the ego, but have to be sought in communal living and interdependence.

No single part can be defined successfully without resorting to the whole. The attitude to life must culminate in one word, "love," if the reference is to a positive interpretation that will ensure spiritual progress. Love in the sense of being all-embracing and willing to sacrifice in conjunction with knowledge and wisdom. It is the only combination to make the ultimate seem attainable - the discovery of eternal truth and the clear and certain perception of Divine Omnipotence.

Now let us examine in detail the individual fundamentals we have mentioned - the soul, the spirit and the body and their relationship to others.

The soul is the vital energy. Its care is the most important basis for the achievement of a healthy attitude to life. But we already know that the soul cannot function on its own - independently of the spirit and body - in earthly existence.

This is the big difference with life in the world beyond. For this reason alone it can be referred to as a more advanced life. It is liberated from the bond of the body and is free in the real sense of the word.

But now let us consider suitable treatment of the soul in combination with the spirit entity in its present state of maturity, disregarding physical handicaps and influences.

Immediately we see that differing energies are in combination here because two spirit entities are hardly ever at the same stage of development.

Spirit entities who have attained an advanced state of development radiate peace and a feeling of well-being whereas spirits who are still at a low state of development have an unpleasant, not to say terrifying influence on their surroundings.

The soul is the seat of the emotions. A positive attitude to life is based on harmonious emotions, which means positive correlations with the spirit and the body. An emotional constitution that tends to exaggeration and does not appreciate beauty and harmony, that indulges in extremes or passively allows the day's events to pass it by is in need of particular care. The spirit entity realises that, above all, the lack of interest in everything beautiful must be redressed and love of music should be fostered. The refinement of the soul under the guidance of the spirit entity is the only way to mature to a harmonious state of balance and create vitality focussed on healthy feelings and love for fellow men.

Abstract teachings are not the best help. Only a good example, be it helpful literature or a person worthy of imitation, will achieve the desired result. The receptive capacity of the soul must be heightened to absorb good influences and deflect bad ones if a healthy approach to life to the benefit of others is really to be achieved. The healthiest body and the accumulation of immense knowledge does not help at all if the soul does not contribute its share of tender emotions.

Next time we will discuss possible ways of doing this.

Perceptions, feelings and love are concepts with endless facets. It is unavoidable that my words are open to various interpretations. But they will all be along the same lines and it is only a matter of greater or lesser degree. There will be many examples in daily life that illustrate how the soul can be cared for. They are not reserved for science only; they are intended for everybody who seeks to progress and is at pains to create a happier existence for himself and all mankind.

Knowledge alone that such paths exist will not lead to the goal. A happy, harmonious state of mind will be the reward for tough and tireless work, the first step towards a correct attitude to life. Tomorrow we continue.

Incorrect interpretation of technical progress. Consequences of inventions and research conducted without feeling.

I NOW want to begin to talk of matters that are of great significance in the lives of people, but have not been accorded proper attention. There is a widespread opinion that feeling is often a hampering influence in life; that it crowds out real thinking and puts matters into a context that damages progress. To give an example: a person has chosen a profession in the field of technology and presumes that the train of thought to be developed and pursued must be quite independent of emotional consideration.

This is precisely why so much damage has been caused by the progress of technology. The exponents of this science, which affects human life so drastically, have never been aware of the fact — and very many are still not aware of it today — that the vital energy of a human being is not a motor but, as I have already said, a very delicate instrument. This must be treated and cared for with the utmost tenderness and consideration. It is pointless to list the achievements which, on account of this one-sided way of thinking, have been discovered and promoted to the detriment rather than the benefit of mankind. And this way of thinking and working still exists today. The realisation has not yet dawned that technology without feeling and consideration for the needs of a healthy life is not only worthless but downright dangerous.

Right now, in this era where technology and its attendant mechanisation reigns supreme, the people who are entrusted with the research and exploitation of technical data must be made aware of the harmonious interplay between spirit and soul. Technology is not progress. It is only a means to promote progress.

We have already noted what should be considered the real progress of mankind — and I must keep repeating it. Matter is not the most desirable goal. It must only figure in a person's range of vision in so far as it is necessary and desirable for a healthy life.

Every technical achievement which is only aimed at giving one person superiority over others without consideration as to whether his personal benefit is to the detriment of his fellow men is to be condemned. It drains the vitality of people. This can only be replaced over a long period of time.

The ethics of technology should be a vital section of the subject matter used for training scientists, scholars and their assistants.

These lessons should begin in schools founded for adults who have already undergone thorough preparatory training. It would not even be necessary to give them these lessons if proper attention had been paid to the care of the soul in childhood. But if adults are correctly trained, many of their children will gain the right attitude and mankind will be shown a way that will lead it in a totally different direction from the one it follows today in the conviction that it is so immensely valuable and absolutely correct.

Let us assume, for example, that people come to the conclusion —after exhaustive examination of the harmful effects of gasses caused by all kinds of engines — that doing without engines would be more beneficial than modifying them, then the time will not be far distant that their manufacture will be severely curtailed.

The technologist must therefore be educated at soul level to test newly developed inventions in order to assess their value to the community. An apparatus which replaces manpower but burdens the operator with a surplus of work and concentration must be discarded as unsuitable. The guideline should be that which allows for easier manipulation and spares vital energy. Minimal exertion and preservation of vitality offers the best results. Or let me express it this way: let people first have their say before they are overwhelmed with new inventions and you will see that much of what is considered desirable by the exponents of technology is expendable.

Whatever is created without true feeling and honest human consideration is created without vital energy. I would say that the soul aspect of the invention is missing because the effect on the human soul has been forgotten. Everything created in exaggerated measure because advantage is taken of all given possibilities, will soon become a superfluous burden to mankind, who will recognise its worthlessness and disruptive consequences.

When I, as a doctor, think how many mistakes, yes, how much harm, has already been caused by the improper use of chemical products because the human soul was considered unimportant and only the existence of the material organism was recognised, then I consider it high time to rectify the error if the damage is not to escalate out of all proportion.

We are not at the dawn of human development; we are close to the middle of it, even though the greater time span still lies ahead of us and we have to come to grips with circumstances as they are.

It is not possible to start afresh on a blank slate. We have to battle to eliminate mistakes and slowly create a bridge to a new life and a proper lifestyle. It is a difficult task, one that certainly cannot be achieved overnight.

It does not matter when a task has to be carried out. It only matters that it has to be done.

Every single person who finds the right path contributes to the transformation of mankind as a whole. From generation to generation progress will be apparent as a start has already been made. Gradually leading spirits on earth are becoming aware of the damage caused by neglecting the spiritual sphere. This is the first step towards recovery.

I will now try to explain exactly how a man's soul is affected when he places an invention at the disposal of his fellow men only for material gain. The initial ideas for the discovery do not stem from the man's own thoughts. Rather, they come from spirits in the world beyond seeking a basis for their work. In such a case it will only dawn on the inventor when he sees his invention at work that its beneficial results, to which he contributed little or nothing, are the advantages it gives people, not the invention itself.

I have especially chosen technology as an example because in this field matter is the major component. The technician, as a rationally working human being, is tempted or is actually at pains to exclude any feelings. This, of course, is a mental process based on his logical appraisal of the work in hand. But as an assignment cannot be undertaken without vital energy, the soul is always involved. It transfers the impulse of will to the brain which has to consider fulfilling the task. If, in so doing, the soul withdraws from the proceedings, the result will be a purely mechanically executed task.

Of course, the exclusion of feeling is often an advantage when a work which is simply material and technical has to be done. But the ultimate goal must never be forgotten: service to fellow men.

Very important technical results are in the main achieved without feeling, which means without consideration for the benefit of mankind. It only remains to hope that such insensitive inventors and researchers are kept in check by good powers.

You have to consider in how far you can trust your feelings to find the correct solution; to know what has to be fostered and what rejected.

As I see it, this is very simple: trust in the good energies in the world beyond. Accept the knowledge they impart, with the honest wish only to do good. Reject all achievements that do not advance the spiritual progress of mankind.

The soul is the link to the spirit world. It is hampered by the wrong concept of life and death. Advice on curing abnormal emotional and mental attitudes.

THE soul as the link to the spirit world and servant of mankind is a subject that will occupy us for a long time. It is not easy for me to describe how it is affected by external influences because the human vocabulary is inadequate and human insight cannot penetrate the inscrutable cosmic energies. Nevertheless I will try to explain how it reacts to a shock or a stimulus, how its reaction is caused and which influences have to be avoided.

The human soul is an organ that defies every earthly concept. It is an organ because everything that functions in the human body is organic even though it is invisible. This could be confusing because medical science makes a clear division between organic and psychic illnesses. Indeed, it does consider that the psyche exists and admits that in the human body there are elements that are not tangible and cannot be measured. But let us not be taken in by this for medical science considers the activity of the soul and spirit only as the effect of organically established fundamentals. The brain is given credit for everything.

For a long time the soul was thought to be situated in the heart, the motor responsible for all living functions. This was not without reason because it is principally this motor which guides and maintains life and its manifestations. But when we reflect that when the heart is quite normal and healthy, life is often terminated by the failure of some other organ, it becomes clear that the soul, or vital energy, is not confined to the heart but, as I have already said, occupies the whole body.

I want to remind you that contact cannot be made with the soul through any one organ, nor can it be cared for and treated through any one organ. A sick organ only indicates that the soul is hampered or ill. It suffices if we understand quite clearly that all organic disturbances - insofar as they are not physically inherited or stem from physical influences - are the result of an improper way of life, an incorrect assessment of its meaning and the pressure of the daily work routine, all of which is not according to our blueprint.

Once again I must remind you that an incorrect assessment of the purpose of life hampers the soul or makes it ill.

A person who mourns the death of a beloved friend or marriage partner and reproaches himself that his conduct towards the deceased was improper, selfish, unfriendly or without the necessary attention or due love, oppresses his soul to the point that can result in his organs not carrying out their proper functions. He is unable to sleep. Instead of quietly gathering strength, his thoughts stray back to the past, causing agitation and discord. The daily routine brings additional problems and stresses with the result that the strength of both the mind and the body steadily drains away.

It may well be that the person who frets and grieves did make mistakes. But to dwell in the past without being able to undo what has been done does not help. The only way to recovery is to learn and adopt the correct attitude to life and death.

He must know that he can speak to his deceased friend or

beloved partner as though he was physically next to him. A single conversation suffices. The realisation of his failure and the wish to recall it will soon bring about the feeling that pardon has been granted.

I have already indicated that careful consideration should be given to any emotions which cause worry so that through analysing and understanding the burden is removed from the soul.

Self-reproach has never been the key to progress. An error which has been committed must be clearly acknowledged and mentally assessed so that it is not repeated. Only the will to do this and nothing else is necessary.

To unburden the soul you must accept that it is not on earth for the last time, but in future lives or in the world beyond will have the possibility of accomplishing what it has neglected to do until now.

In actual fact it is not the soul that has failed; it is the personality, the spirit entity. But in incarnate opinion the two are so closely allied that it is difficult to decide whether the manifestations are mental or emotional. Let us therefore accept that those which we consider to be emotional are indeed so.

In the treatment and alleviation of such modes of behaviour it is immaterial whether it is caused by the spirit entity or the soul. To look ahead, not back, in the knowledge that what has been is only a criterion which, once recognised, offers the possibility of a change for the better, is already a step towards a positive attitude to life.

On the other hand, you must not think that it is unimportant to seek progress in this life because you still have numerous ones to follow. I don't want my comforting explanation to be misunderstood.

Do not be discouraged because a wrong action weighs heavy on your conscience. Rather learn from your mistakes, decide to do better in future and avoid hatred, envy and other negative thoughts. Only then will you find relief from the oppressive burden.

But if you persist in incorrect tactics or mistaken self-justification, the burden imposed on your soul will only intensify. Knowledge of life after incarnate death is part of your good resolve. I will remind you of it when we consider the successful treatment of a sick soul. So much for today.

MESSAGES FROM A DOCTOR IN THE FOURTH DIMENSION

The cultivation of art is a significant component of a healthy philosophy of life. Definition of "art."

I URGE you to pay attention to the subjects I dealt with yesterday and follow my advice. Do not gloss over what I wrote. It was not meant merely to satisfy intellectual curiosity. These new ideas must penetrate your soul and fill it to the extent that it creates a new basis on which to build further.

I am very anxious to see how you accept my words and whether my expectations will be realised. Take your time. It is not easy. A concept of life that has been inculcated or simply accepted for very many years cannot so radically be altered that ideas have to be immediately turned upside down.

Do not be impatient. Bear with me. There is still much more to learn and change. We are only at the beginning. The school I invite you to attend is difficult but rewarding. You will not regret following my train of thought.

Today I will go one step further and try to explain what has to be done when people devote all their energy to earning their daily bread and don't find the time to nuture and develop their own personality.

Most people measure their success in terms of material achievement and yet find no satisfaction in their accomplishments. But there are others who realise that they have a soul which makes its requirements quite clear. They feel the need to occupy themselves with or simply enjoy beautiful, inspirational matters that stimulate them both mentally and emotionally and are free of material considerations and fulfilment.

The realisation that matter burdens and chains the soul gives them the incentive to achieve goals in spheres which have nothing to do with the maintenance of their existence, but vitalize their physical powers to such an extent that they are happy and content.

Above all, this comes from art. Not everybody is an artist. Only a few are given the talent to produce works of art. But they are not allowed to create them for themselves; they are charged to employ their powers and skills for the benefit and pleasure of their fellow men. Just as the artist is obliged to serve humanity with his art, so people at large are obliged to recognise him, to make his art their own and turn it to account in their soul and spirit.

Art is not a hobby for the few, but one of the fundamentals given to mankind for the attainment of a more elevated level of life in the material world.

Creative work is part of a positive philosophy. It may not be scorned, nor may it be disregarded or considered superfluous just because it is not absolutely necessary for the preservation of existence.

Life is not just a matter of caring for the material body and keeping it healthy through attention and nourishment. A spirit that strives to progress must be fostered so that his advance to a better and higher development is assured.

Many a pleasant occupation is condemned as unprofitable when in reality it is of much greater use to mankind than technical achievements.

It is not wasteful when a person who lives in extremely modest circumstances chooses to spend his personal income on music or the theatre instead of on eating and drinking. How many good books are unread because money is not spent on buying them. Clothes and jewellery in exaggerated measure are considered more important than the development of spirit and soul.

Admittedly it is very difficult to decide what is true art and where the boundary lies between soulless handicraft and a God-given gift. It is an extremely delicate feeling which is not generally inherent, but, as in every profession, is confined to those with a vocation. Even if they are not creatively engaged they are still experts in some artistic area and can very well decide between what is or is not art. Artists are few and far between if art is restricted to creatively inclined or inspired people.

Art is also the interpretation and explanation of works whose purpose is not apparent to everybody.

Every human soul has the need to enjoy beauty, melodious sound or sublime thoughts, but not all at the same time. Yet the acquisition of a positive attitude to life means that none of these areas may be neglected.

Above all it is music that affects the soul most. If it is really divinely inspired, it can heal those who are sick or have gone astray. It is the very best way of uplifting agitated souls, transposing them to higher spheres and giving them an idea of the wonderful sounds they will hear one day in a better world.

Music is the basis of existence in higher spheres. As the human spirit develops, it will increasingly become the cornerstone in the rearing and formation of young people. As present this may be difficult to believe because mankind's development is still relatively primitive. Progress is not to be reckoned from one generation to the next. It can only be perceived in the course of many hundreds of years or more.

Nevertheless, every person is obliged to work towards this higher form of development. Nobody should accept the current state of affairs simply because he cannot see any results for himself and his children.

The cultivation of art is therefore a very important part of a healthy philosophy of life and care is certainly taken that for every person, even the weakest and least developed, there is an appealing and suitable opening in some area. Art is not only what a certain individual can do better than the majority in one or other field. It is quite simply that which in purity and nobility affects the soul through form, colour or tone and is not brought about mechanically without the influence of the soul and spirit.

Of course, one could classify all shapely things as artistic creations. If you see those created many thousands of years ago when mankind was at a far lower stage of development than today, it was certainly art.

Today the concept "art" must be judged from a more exacting point of view. A truly artistic creation cannot be produced without intelligence and conscious will; it must have a particular stamp which only the personality can bring forth.

Now comes the question: is man able to create a true work of art without help? What is a true work of art? The answer is: one that never loses its value. Its high standing remains for all time, even when tastes and viewpoints have altered.

Really great masterpieces, in the field of music for instance, are never produced by the artist alone. I have mentioned that such people are mediums who absorb the pure, heavenly tones and according to their emotional abilities, receptiveness, spiritual maturity and technical formation, reproduce these to the best of their ability. This vocation is not for their own benefit and pleasure. All mankind must profit from their works and enjoy them. I will continue to remind you of this: take care that art, good literature, music and every edifying occupation is not neglected. All are important milestones on the road towards a positive attitude to life.

MESSSAGES FROM A DOCTOR IN THE FOURTH DIMENSION

Attitude to life is not a product of philosophical planning, but rather a style of living and adaption of the given fundamentals. The error of religions.

THERE will still be many a chapter linked to the subject "attitude to life." In due course, I want to examine everything that has a positive influence on its formation.

I have dealt with art and named music as a prevalent factor. We have also learned that mental activity is not a dominating force. The soul plays a certain role in the deliberation, decision and assessment of undertakings in the interest of everybody. But the well-being of the entire community should first be taken into consideration. Only then may the ambition of an inventor, for instance in the field of technology, be satisfied. These are fundamentals which are essential for the welfare not only of the individual but also for the entire nation.

On account of his free will man is able to interpret matters quite independently although, as in every mental activity, he is either aided or hampered by material essentials. This does not only apply to his immediate environment but to his attitude to people in general.

The criteria in this case are the acceptance or rejection of the standards set by the people around him as well as habits based on custom and law. Part of a positive outlook is a person's endeavour to accept the latter and make use of all available possibilities to improve the well-being of his fellow-men and help create better conditions for the next generation.

A positive approach to life is not the result of a deliberate philosophical project. It is a life-style based on immediate reactions to important questions and events on which the individual has to take a standpoint.

How often have we altered, or had to alter our opinion, either because of our own experiences or as a result of significant changes in the way of life and the environment allotted to us?

Life forms peoples' ideas and gives them the opportunity of free determination. Of course, as I have already mentioned, every such determination is dependent on the spiritual maturity and receptivity of the soul.

Accordingly, every opinion on the meaning of life must vary.
Above all, we want to determine which influences could be of

importance for the majority of people; which fundamentals exist, which must be created and which paths must be followed.

The goal is the conviction that only a life of friendly intercourse is worth striving for, that there are many paths to this end and that the necessary education can be obtained in many ways. The correct training of a child is to condition it to accept this principle in later years.

Egotism is a major drawback. It impedes the education of young people and makes it very difficult for them to become helpful.

A man who has been reared to believe that he has only to care for himself and his own well-being will most probably not develop a sense of fellowship.

A healthy existence based on a harmonious balance is the very best guideline for youngsters. For we are just not able to master our fate alone.

We discussed this subject in an earlier chapter and concluded that all spirit entitities who today are endeavouring to progress in all spheres, from those of obscurity to those of overwhelming radiance, will one day flow into one single light. But a lone spirit, separated from the community, can never attain this goal.

Of course, this knowledge is familiar to an enlightened spirit. He accepts it as an irrefutable truth and a necessary condition for attaining his goal. In its different religions mankind has accepted this basic truth as the most important commandment because the tenets of eternal life have been known and imparted by good spirits for many thousands of years. But due to the influence of matter, greed and the unfair distribution of worldly goods, people have strayed far from this timeless reality.

Their judgement of things and people is only based on outward appearances. They have forgotten inner values; forgotten how to promote them and raise them far above external values. By this I do not mean to laud the return to religious communities. On the contrary. Through the arrogance of so many sects and exaggerated religious practices a very understandable rejection has gained considerable ground and prepared the way for a totally opposite situation.

It is also vital that the Church — no matter of which confession — moves away from these exaggerated religious practices. It should not support the viewpoints that only a person who devotes himself to religion is good, noble and orgained by God in word or deed. Rather there should be an approximation of views which meet halfway.

A life devoted to the community was, for a long time, regarded as the privilege of religious orders. It was linked to the renunciation of all material pleasures and in the opinion of just about the entire world was regarded as an expiatory sacrifice on the part of such people. However, they saw it as a renunciation of the world to preserve their souls for a higher life, mainly out of fear of a non-existent hell. The idea of serving the community thereby became a travesty.

Community life does not mean total denial and subordination to the demands and wishes of others, even in an emergency. It is another form of assistance, of personal dedication to one's fellow men with consideration, attention and willingness to help and make sacrifices.

Everybody can live for, and with, the community. It requires no deprivation of personal wishes, no consideration that earthly necessities are unworthy.

It is part of a sound attitude to life that in the same measure that you avail yourself of earthly goods to enjoy them you do not begrudge your fellow-men equal pleasure. Be prepared to help and serve in love without infringing your own personality.

Service that escalates into subservience is not a sign of goodness, but of weakness. A healthy gauge is therefore needed to find the right measure which is why it is necessary to educate people to this end from early childhood; to open their eyes and guide them with reasoned arguments and convincing examples to a blessed and self-enrichening attitude towards their fellow men.

Life in and for the community will occupy our attention further, as there are still very many points of contact and several problems which every thinking person will be glad to have explained.

Some thoughts about making a living.
The community and society.

I HAVE not yet exhausted the subject of the proper attitude towards other people as the essential condition for a correct approach to life. There are still many facets I have to discuss.

A suitable philosophy embraces not only the conviction of eternal life and Divine Omnipotence, but also a personal opinion about earthly existence with its civilisation and everyday demands.

It is a vast subject, but I will explain some of the most important aspects, especially the attitude towards making a living.

Everybody has his own concept of obligations and rights and strives to master them in his own way. As no two people are at the same stage of spiritual development, there is no set way to go about this. But one factor applies to everybody: the necessity of earning the right to worldly goods through work; of proving your own worth and not obliging your fellow men to be responsible for your maintenance.

Unfortunately I have established that there are many people in the world who live in slavery, even though the term is no longer in use. It doesn't matter what a system is called, only what effect it has. Sad, if one considers the many institutions in the world constructed by manpower with total disregard for the personal freedom of the individual and for the use of only a few. It is always the mistaken attitude to matter, the craving for possessions and power that turns people into monsters. This, in general, affects the masses, sometimes even a whole nation.

But just as the wrong attitude towards people in general cannot bring permanent results, it will have similar repercussions on the individual's relations with his colleagues at work.

Subordinates and superiors in professional life must be equal on a human level; the difference only lies in their achievements.

Subordination in professional matters should not degenerate into subservience nor should this be demanded by superiors.

Where people are judged according to a different yardstick on account of their background and a so-called higher education, no harmony, and therefore no progress, can be expected. The principal rule for co-operation in professional life is that everybody be accorded respect and consideration if the collaboration is to produce the desired results. In this field too the help from the world beyond is important. The head of a company who is receptive to the guidance of good spirits will rarely encounter enemies in his organisation.

The far too rapid development of technology with its impersonal and - I would say - arrogant attitude towards the powers beyond the earthly sphere results in scant regard for human existence. It causes general denial of eternal values and of the bond with Divine

Omnipotence which is so absolutely necessary for the spirit and soul, so that it is to be feared that all these great technical achievements brought about without universal love and consideration for the community as a whole will one day disappear again.

It is really a sacrilege that spiritual abilities are used so inconsiderately in all possible spheres simply for the gratification of a craving for power. Humanity has forgotten humility, which should be the guiding star in all undertakings, no matter in which field.

Once again I wish to point out that professional people who seek satisfaction and happiness in their work must consider a positive approach to life and a conscious, clear concept of the purpose and necessity of their labour.

I would have to write a lengthy treatise for whoever seeks detailed explanations about this. But it is not the purpose of my messages. I only want to mention the fundamentals for a positive attitude to life. Exhaustive treatment would require that all the positive and negative components would have to be considered.

I must add one more observation to this. A profession is seldom a calling, particularly not when it is manual, mechanical labour. This will never provide the satisfaction that a soul and spirit requires to progress. In this case it is necessary to find an additional interest which offsets the monotony and vacuum of the daily grind. But the knowledge that manual labour provides a certain, suitable standard of life creates a sense of duty and a satisfaction that the salary earned is commensurate with the work that has been done and has not been received undeservedly. A sense of duty makes a person strong and free and establishes a right to cheerfulness and happiness. A task done without joy brings no results. But a task executed to a maximum of ability brings blessings; there is no saying when and in what form. And this, even though at the time, his exertions seemed to have gone unnoticed.

Man is not in a position to recognise all the reactions to his deeds. Often, what appears to be a stroke of luck out of a clear blue sky is perhaps the reward for past achievements.

I am not empowered to reveal all the secrets about the correlations with the world beyond, but I can say that even in the smallest and most modest undertakings cosmic energies are at work in accordance with the eternal divine laws.

But nobody should rely on the saying that man alone does not direct his fate. His will is free. If he has positive intentions which are in the interest of his fellow men and are unfettered by thoughts of power and greed, he only attracts good, helpful spirits. This is always, of course, subject to the condition that he goes to work with a clear conscience.

All these aspects amount to the fact that nobody can lead a happy life without consideration for his fellow men and the community.

But not only the community binds people together. Society must also be given some thought. Whereas in the community there is no class distinction, society is classified according to material viewpoints. Background, education and physical abilities like sport and so on are the qualifications for the establishment of various social strata. This requires careful consideration and affects the community. As long as society is not prepared to judge people regardless of their background, environment and education, justice and everything that influences peoples' lives will be subject to many errors.

Spiritual maturity does not go hand in hand with a person's background and education. This is the cause of mistakes that occur in the world, brought about by leaders who are not leaders, but who dominate the masses because they have the ability to hold them spellbound. Nevertheless, for the present the world would be unthinkable without social order. At least it offers people the opportunity of meeting others with similar interests and enjoying their company. There will, however, be changes; in fact, they have already begun in that material fundamentals - by this I mean material possessions - are no longer the qualifying factor for higher education.

I have already mentioned that an advanced spirit is often incarnated in a humble environment because material possessions are more apt to hinder than further his development. As soon as this realisation becomes general knowledge, society will pull down the barriers and choose the best people to guide humanity.

Personal judgement, courage and self-confidence as the basis for re-adjusting to a sound attitude to life.

THERE are still many aspects of a sound attitude to life that I have to touch on. They will help smooth the way and ensure people a goal which permits them to adhere to the rules they have resolved to follow in their everyday life.

Rules like this only make sense if they are equally applicable to everybody, not only to oneself, and do not require particular maturity, experience or academic education. They are basic attitudes, guided by the desire to only do good and act correctly.

In the same way that the individual has either a positive or negative attitude to life, so too do nations or groups of people linked together by common interests.

The philosophy of life of a nation is reflected in its politics and its attitude towards other countries. It is embodied in the few who come to power one way or another and win the confidence of the masses. These leaders often have a philosophy of life for themselves and their immediate circle, which is good. But frequently they are the tools of powers opposed to their striving for truth and justice.

In this era of such great contrasts it is probably difficult to establish a basis where only positive energies predominate and there are no negative influences. The ideal would be to find a person or a group who prove to be guided by all-embracing love and selfless devotion. But who could test them? How would they recognise such virtues?

I just wanted to make it clear that it is not possible to realise such a dream while the majority of people, or at least those in a position of power in government circles, do not have a sound outlook on life.

Let us therefore put this matter aside and instead concentrate on the individual who must and will one day achieve this dream of dreams through free will.

Now I want to recapitulate the fundamental rules.

In the first place there must be the correct attitude towards the links between the material world and the entire universe with its infinite values and energies. Then comes the correct assessment of matter and material possessions; one's right to them and the obligation to treat them only as a means to an end and not as an end in itself. This positions the individual both in the universe and on earth.

There follows the reflection: what is the purpose of earthly existence for man? According to the eternal, irrefutable laws he has to strive to progress and finally attain eternal bliss together with all the other spirit entities working towards the same goal. He cannot avoid this progress nor the fact that the end purpose must be achieved through personal free will. This is the chief element in every spirit entity. Free will allows a person to formulate his outlook on life, revise it and live and work accordingly.

To determine the worth of everything around him, to have his own free judgement, quite independent of any other opinion, is of great importance for developing his way of life. This also includes the ability to recognise in which matters freedom of action is permitted and when and in which way it is necessary to exercise caution or to adapt.

I cannot establish guidelines, even if these could help the majority of people. Such a perfect scheme would be nothing short of spiritual coercion. A harmonious balance attained by calm deliberation will help most people to find a suitable way of life. Of course, by "most people" I mean the majority of those who have chosen to progress or at least are trying to do so.

A sound attitude to life also requires courage; this means unshakeable confidence in yourself even when it becomes abundantly clear that you have made an enormous mistake. Learn from your errors. Don't brood over them. Shake off negative feelings. Set to work with the firm resolve to make amends. It suffices that life be differently interpreted and the correct adjustment will follow.

Let us assume that a person who has always considered great wealth and material riches the most desirable goals now, through my teaching, comes to the conclusion that he must change his way of life. He will not suddenly renounce everything he has acquired, give it away or let it go to ruin. This would be quite wrong. But if his intentions are sincere, he will pave the way for it to be used for the benefit of the community and will soon realise how much inner freedom and happiness it brings him. The mere planning of such a change would prove me right. The fear that ingratitude will often be all he will receive for his goodness and generosity should not frighten him off. This is not the criterion for success. It is vested in his own personality.

The subject of the various components leading to a positive view of life is not exhausted. But I wanted to get away from just listing the various issues and have therefore digressed from the theme. I apologise for this but hope that I have presented a practical view of the matter which will prove useful to many readers.

I close for today because I think the various ideas have to be explored individually. But this will be too much for one chapter and will make excessive demands on my medium.

MESSSAGES FROM A DOCTOR IN THE FOURTH DIMENSION

The value and advantage of knowledge and wisdom.

TODAY I want to continue where I left off yesterday. Everybody has his own idea about life and cannot put it aside and adopt a new one immediately as if he were putting on and taking off his clothes. Such a re-orientation requires great patience. Patience with oneself and understanding and forgiveness, which I have already mentioned.

I must remind you to re-read the chapters and paragraphs dealing with this subject. Like a circle in which man is the central pivot the ideas, opinions and interpretations about the needs of life are ranged as markers along the upward path from the base. They will guide you onwards. A well rounded picture emerges. Every requirement, every conviction aspired to is equidistant from the viewpoint of the beholder, the person who is sincerely striving to make progress. Every one is essential and equally important for the desired result.

No reasonable point of view may be ignored. Harmony will never be achieved if every facet is not clearly seen and understood.

Several concepts and ground rules essential to our overall picture are still missing so I am going to deal with them in this chapter.

First of all, I want to mention the effort to obtain knowledge and wisdom. It is essential for everybody to make this effort, although the degree may vary. I have already pointed out that knowledge alone may not be the ultimate goal. Only knowledge applied, and by this I mean knowledge put to work, in the interest and for the benefit of mankind represents the fulfilment of a task which a person has undertaken. And such a task cannot be divided, allowing part of it to be done in this life and the remainder in a later life. It is almost certain that progress would be retarded in such a case.

Whoever comes to earth with the wish to advance and qualify himself for a higher sphere must always take this basic rule into consideration.

Now there are certainly careers and fields of knowledge, for example the various branches of science, where it is not easy to see how the community may be served, but there is actually not a single one whose purpose is not to benefit it. Practically all of them are directly related to life and to the laws of civilisation and culture. They have to do with the requirements of a healthy, progressive existence and as such they are the basis and promotion of knowledge.

To some extent, knowledge already attained is being used for the creation of new forms of life; to some extent research work is being undertaken to derive from the cosmos and all the available energies new possibilities to make earthly existence more comfortable for people. But how much more worthwhile all these undertakings would be if the underlying thoughts came from another direction, namely the one I suggest, and the main attention was not directed to the success, the fame and the credit of the individual.

How many great inventions, discoveries and beneficial results of scientific research remain unused simply because one person wants to steal a march on the next so that no progress is made in these fields? They are either lost to humanity or it will only benefit from them at a far later date. Increased commitment to mankind would have led to far greater progress: a much sounder and more valuable basis for life would have been achieved a long time ago. Unfortunately this is the case in all fields of science and not least in medecine. Here there must be radical changes.

We have also differentiated between knowledge and wisdom. Admittedly, the former gives rise to the latter, but it is only a fraction of what the word "wisdom" should convey. And this brings us once again to all-embracing love, which is part of a sound outlook on life.

Wisdom is the application of knowledge, but only in the best sense, with all the positive energies. I only wish to speak of that wisdom which is attainable on earth and is - as I have said - in no way comparable to the wisdom which, in the world beyond, leads to absolute perfection. It implies the discovery of the ultimate truths which both man and we spirit entities who are already more enlightened are still endlessly far removed from.

But if we nevertheless allow this concept validity for those on earth, we must at least stipulate that mere knowledge and the soulless accumulation of experiences and information are not sufficient to acquire wisdom. The soul must play a significant role here, not as mere vital energy, but in its capacity to react emotionally. Such feeling must decide what value and benefit can be attributed to each piece of knowledge before the memory is burdened with it.

There are many scholars who graduate and then rush headlong into a new field and begin to study all over again, acquiring more knowledge without having put into practice what they have already learned. It may be possible that after graduation a person finds these studies which he was made to believe were promising — always in the material sense, of course — are not in accordance with his plans. Therefore, he courageously starts again. But this is only justifiable and of intrinsic worth if the wish to serve other people is the decisive factor. In every other case it is a total misinterpretation of the ultimate value of knowledge and generally, the inability to face the tasks of life fearlessly and resolutely. Mankind will never benefit from his learning and the person himself, so stubbornly obsessed with his craving for knowledge, will hardly derive pleasure from his work.

My comments refer to the sciences and the knowledge that can be derived from them. But there are other areas in human existence where knowledge and wisdom can be obtained. It is not always necessary to engage in academic studies which nowadays do not fulfil the expectations — at least not in most cases — that would be desirable for the requirements of research and progress.

Let us consider people who neither read nor write books; who gather their practical knowledge and experiences from their close ties to nature and are humble and unpretentious. How much knowledge and wisdom they often have! In their closeness to nature they have preserved a far less troubled and purer emotional life than people who live in confined quarters. They recognise human shortcomings and willingly and thankfully shelter under Divine Providence. In their tranquillity they find the time and leisure to get to know peoples' characters. In their isolation they are much more dependent on reciprocal help than a person in a big city. At least they are intensely aware of the necessity of it. Because of this they create a genuine community. Without having to think about it, they know how one person is in duty bound to stand in for his neighbour.

To be sure, modern technology has also made unpleasant inroads here causing a so-called beneficial set of circumstances which appear to have brought unbelievable progress but will, in the end, prove detrimental to these healthy people living close to nature.

The assessment of human qualities in the study of character. A justifiable or exaggerated desire to gain recognition.

ONCE again, let us search out new aspects which contribute to a positive attitude to life.

The goal is unchanged, but a few words are not sufficient to describe the correlations and this is important if they are to be understood and applied.

This is why it is necessary to examine all the human qualities that together constitute a personality. Are they good or bad, kindhearted or indifferent, egotistical or altruistic, unpretentious or avaricious, reserved or obtrusive?

If we examine these differences and realise how many levels and degrees there are of each quality, we will have cause to reflect that — as I have already mentioned — what applies to one does not apply to all. People cannot be judged by one yardstick. So it is in learning about the personality of your fellow men, in probing the character of the people you meet.

In the first instance we attempt to judge others according to our own qualities, or at least compare their character traits and implications with our own. This is only of value if we try to establish a fair opinion and find out whether, in one or other quality, the other person is superior or inferior. And this is precisely where the correct interpretation must be made. An opinion should be formed without condemnation. There must only be the wish to understand and define it within the framework of the overall personality.

We have already discussed knowledge of human nature and how important it is for the individual to learn to judge himself. It is vital for your daily contact with other people for, without understanding and forgiveness, without weighing up personalities in their entirety, a social life is neither successful nor beneficial.

At this point we must examine the desire to assert oneself, which everybody should possess to a certain extent.

A person with no wish to gain recognition and prove his worth is without aspiration, resourceless and totally lacking in willpower. He will drift along apathetically, live for the day, attach himself like a parasite to other people and adapt himself more or less to their way of life.

It is in the natural, inherent instinct of man to have the ambition to make his mark, to accomplish something in one or othere sphere of life. If he is not predestined for brain work and does not have the ability to prove his worth in this field, he will concentrate on physical work and not be satisfied until he has mastered it.

The same principle that applies in all other fields, does so here. The middle path is the correct one to follow. Make yourself respected where it is justified; always with modesty but with quiet determination. The obstacles that man encounters in every situation in life can only be mastered by a healthy desire to assert himself. Difficulties are there to be overcome. The person who rightly realises that he must not be intimidated, who will not allow himself to be deflected from his purpose, will make himself respected and reach his intended goal. His self-respect will compel him to do so; he will have a definite feeling as to what extent he may assert himself.

But in this respect he often acts against his inner voice and invests more energy than is really necessary to overcome an obstacle. An exaggerated drive for personal prestige causes him to overdo his efforts. Mistaken ambition will give him satisfaction, but never bring grist to his mill. The result is bitter disappointment and frustration. It is unnecessary to quote examples. Everybody is familiar with such cases, either through personal experience or unfortunate episodes at every level of society.

A sound attitude encompasses a person's ability to know his proper station in life. Everybody can acquire this ability. It only requires a conscientious examination of his own disposition. Of course, this necessitates a healthy soul which sees matters clearly and in the right light. A handicapped soul will underrate its own ability and because of this will either resign itself or, knowing that it might fail, overshoot the mark and, without proper control and deliberation, battle for recognition where it is neither necessary nor advantageous.

In my medical practice I often had to intervene in cases where this applied. Only after many words of encouragement and careful, sympathetic probing into the patient's soul could I help renew the energy which gave totally erroneous thoughts free passage to the correct goal.

A person who does not strive for personal recognition can experience disastrous consequences. These often lead to total resignation, even suicide.

Going to extremes is not part of a healthy outlook on life, but it is one way to underline the importance of asserting oneself.

In children this desire reveals itself much more noticeably than in adults. You should not consider it a shortcoming or a bad character trait and try to suppress it. This striving for recognition must only be properly guided: the results of setting goals which might cause disappointments must be made apparent. Only personal experience should determine the child's guidelines and not suppression, denial or strict punishment.

The constant pressure of daily existence obliges the adult to pay far more attention to asserting himself and weaving these concepts into his life. He must acquire the ability to examine himself from a higher point of view and in honest self-criticism seek to discover the adequacy, exaggeration or insufficient care accorded to his personal importance. It is a degree of self-education, a judgement of oneself, and is only successful if it is undertaken in an honest manner.

I am compelled to set important tasks for those who are willing to follow my train of thought and apply it. Do not weaken or despair if the correct approach to the matter is not found immediately. Man is not free from error or should I say nobody is free from error. But this is precisely the basis for success because the battle against error is gradual, confident progress.

With this, we have placed one more little stone in our mosaic and can be on the look-out for new ones. I still have much to tell you. I hope you look forward to my messages.

The courage to face the truth and the hampering effect of one's upbringing and environment.

IF I speak of a positive outlook on life, a subject that so many scholars, philosophers and other experts in this field have studied so closely, I feel it almost an imposition to add to what has already been explained.

But you will have to admit that there is a small difference. On earth, with materialistic ways of considering matters, concepts are often somewhat altered, sometimes turned back to front. This is, of course, because life on earth is considered to be the ultimate and only one granted just for the short human time-span. What is missing is the more far-seeing approach, the higher standpoint from which matters must be considered if you want to move closer to the truth.

To this must be added that as a doctor I take into account all the medical aspects as well as the reflections of neurologists and psychiatrists. In my earlier messages I explained in detail how much the soul, which the doctor has to take into consideration when administering treatment, is dependent on daily circumstances, the interpretation of the purpose of life and all the elements which could affect this point of view. It is, therefore, not like an organic illness or an operation where only the body has to be considered. But — and this is more difficult — the psychiatrist has to study in his own individual way the reactions caused by environment and custom and find out the intangible influences on the soul and spirit.

I mention all these influences on the soul because both they and the resulting conditions are still generally under-estimated.

I said that in the case of organic illnesses only the body had to be taken into consideration. This was not intended as a contradiction to my emphatically expressed teaching that every organic illness has its origin in a sick or handicapped soul. By this I meant that in the case of an organic illness the physical body alone was to be examined because the sick organ is visible, tangible, measurable and yes, it can be removed.

The search for the cause is secondary. I repeat this to jog your memory and avoid misunderstanding.

In fact, everything I say is so clear and nothing new to most people. Yet I know that this subject will only be fully understood if we base our study on the fundamental importance of the soul.

How many people never think of tracing the reason for a failure to an incorrect attitude towards the case in question but instead go to great lengths to shift the blame everywhere else to clear their conscience? They lie to themselves instead of giving the matter serious attention and finding the courage to face the truth.

Learn from your mistakes: don't hold others responsible for them. In most cases the causes lie within yourself. Think carefully, then everything will be quite clear and there will be no mistakes.

Courage to face the truth is also part of a positive attitude to life. Everybody knows the difference between right and wrong and whether he has acted incorrectly in a certain situation. He has only to use this ability to think the matter over and examine everything affecting it in a positive and objective way. This requires a degree of bravery because a weak spirit and an unfit soul often do not have the strength to bear the burden brought on by recognising and admitting an error and cannot find a way to corrrect it.

Think back to your own childhood. Perhaps you were up to some mischief but would not admit it. You sought to justify yourself in your own eyes, often not because of fear of punishment but simply because of a feeling of shame. Children seldom have the courage to admit to mistakes, inattention or carelessness. Those who do are usually the ones who have been educated early on to its benefits. They have been guided to learn from their mistakes.

Of course, I do not refer to malicious characteristics with which we are not going to deal here.

The ability to face the truth can greatly progress a person who is unstable, cannot think or act for himself and has never expressed a personal opinion. This is often the case where there is overwhelming reliance, in the material sense, on people around.

A child who grows up in a bad environment, surrounded from the very beginning by dishonest, lying, even thieving people will, at first, consider this way of life the proper one and display the same characteristics. Gradually the knowledge dawns that other people have a different, totally opposite, attitude and condemn his. Such a child needs great courage to react to his surroundings, to re-learn and face the truth. This is an extreme example because of the confrontation of concepts and attitudes which acutally has to be experienced.

In every sphere of human life there are incorrect interpretations which are often very difficult to put aside.

Courage to face the truth means freeing the soul from this heavy burden. Therefore, it is part of the blueprint for life.

In a case like this the psychiatrist, who must recognise such influences and shortcomings, must awaken in the patient the response of facing and dealing with matters both in a positive and negative sense.

I consider positive, the battle against feelings of inferiority, negative, the overestimation of oneself. The latter climaxes in finding fault with others if an undertaking does not succeed or a wish is not realised.

That a foreign influence can cause a failure is, of course, possible, but an unstable, uncertain character will only seek to find the fault in himself and despair rather than accept that a stroke of fate has prevented the successful outcome of an issue. And while I mention fate I want to add that for decisions of vital significance in the life of a person, free will is not the only factor; the blueprint also plays a role.

Here the courage to face the truth is of great importance. Let me quote an example: a person is on the threshold of a career that promises financial security for life, but he is certain that he is not suited to the work. He knows it will never bring him happiness and contentment. If he lacks the pluck to decide against it because those around him would not agree and be displeased with him, the matter will become an emotional burden and lead to severe depression. At this stage it would be difficult to establish the reason for his agitated condition. Initially he lacked the courage to choose the path which his judgement had decided on. Now he will certainly shrink from putting his cards on the table.

Let everyone write "Courage to face the truth" on the first page of his diary. If he doesn't have one, let him repeat these words every morning before he decides on the do's and don'ts for the day.

It is unnecessary to state that you must not lie to your fellow men. It is a foregone conclusion. But it is often much more dangerous to lie to yourself. In any case, it is very unwise. Nevertheless, everybody who reads these lines will weigh these words and come to the conclusion that in his life too such mistakes have been made. Often.

But don't cling to the past. Think ahead and do better!

Living together in the family.

TODAY we are going to discuss important aspects of family life.

We have spoken about the individual's position in relation to himself and within the community, but the smallest circle of the community, the family, has not yet been dealt with. Here, as in other spheres, there are basic principles and laws that have to be observed.

In the course of the last few centuries there have been many changes in family relationships to both the benefit and detriment of the people concerned.

To begin with we must establish which family members we are

dealing with. Some would consider a smaller, some, a larger circle.

For our study I do not wish to include the numerous forbears and the many aunts, nephews and cousins.

Family, in the purest sense of the word, is parents and children. And even for this smallest of circles there is a long list of fundamentals and rules to observe for an ideal life together.

The family is the basis for community life. It is the first step, the good example for the harmonious union of all people, the family of nations, as the saying does.

But we are far removed from this ideal condition. How many families can state that they enjoy a life of purest harmony?

Let us begin our study with the two people who are responsible for a good family life. The parents.

In a family, feeling should be predominant in all matters of daily life. This is extremely important. Perhaps you have a task to fulfil which you consider essential, but if it affects or disturbs the rhythm of daily life, for instance it damages the health of family members or casts some other burden on them, you must consider whether it would not be better to renounce the benefits of the task in favour of harmony. Consideration is therefore one of the main requisites for parents. Consideration towards each other but most of all, consideration towards their children.

The correct philosophy of life for parents implies the conviction, or should I say the knowledge, that they have to be there for their children and may not, simply on account of their physical superiority, consider that their children have to be grateful for their existence and therefore have to respect them in a manner that resembles submission to a foreign will.

It is a matter that requires careful consideration. I have often pointed out that parents have every reason to thank the Eternal Almighty that a spirit entity has been entrusted to them and that they may, with love and the greatest care, guide this child until it has attained worldly maturity. Spiritual maturity was granted to it at birth. Often, this is to a far greater degree than to its parents.

This knowledge, together with the awareness of the great commitment they have accepted, is part of the right attitude to life for parents.

Parents who are wise and have the best of intentions towards their children will show them the greatest consideration in daily life.

The children will reciprocate, for a good example is, and remains, the best teacher.

The demand for consideration — which is often made as a matter of course to children because Father has come home tired from work and needs his rest and so on — is a far greater mistake than parents can imagine. According to them, well-brought up children do not speak at table, particularly when adults are talking. This does not make for harmony in family life, but rather a household of those who dominate and those who are dominated.

I could follow this up with a lesson as to what to say and do according to the individual daily occurrences. But this goes decidedly too far and becomes superfluous once parents consider their children equal partners and, either after due consideration, or uncertainty as to their spiritual maturity, talk to them as they would to adults.

There are so many matters in daily life that an uninhibited, childish spirit can deal with more effectively and appropriately than an adult. How much security and self-confidence is given a child when its opinion is requested! Do not believe that it becomes presumptuous on this account. It is much more likely to realise early on how difficult it is in life always to make the correct decision. Many a mistake will soon teach it to become a very modest but self-confident person.

It is neither right nor necessary that a father, awarded the custody of his children by law, should exercise it with force. Custody merely reminds him of his important commitment.

A right attitude to life within the family circle includes a sense of dependence on one another and the significant obligation to vouch for one another in all situations. There is nothing more precious, nothing finer, than when a person can say that in his father, son, brother or mother he has a friend in whom he can confide his innermost thoughts.

Trust does not come automatically as a family right. It has to be earned, regardless of the relationship. That it is most easily found within the family circle where a harmonious contact between parents and children offers the possibility, is readily understandable, but unfortunately this is seldom the case. This is because children in the main see their parents as strict disciplinarians who are far from being the friends they ought to be.

People who in their interpretation of the purpose of earthly existence have included marriage and family and therefore wish to do justice to the propagation of mankind, must include the correct conduct towards their children in their programme for life. They must learn, and in most cases will have to re-learn, since they so often think that what they have experienced and how their parents treated them is the correct way to treat their own children. Admittedly, their own education followed an established pattern, but they should remember that once parental influence came to an end, a form of self-education had to take over. The obligation exists to put aside prejudices which evolved from an incorrect upbringing. If this has hampered spontaneous development, it must be replaced by a personal view of life.

Let us now consider the children and the results of a good, harmonious family life, and the opposite.

I have explained that every child must be given the opportunity to discover its blueprint for life and develop along the lines it has undertaken to follow. A child which grows up in loving surroundings will easily do this. Now I want to point out why I wish to confine the family only to parents and children.

It is unforgiveable to hand a child around and seek praise and approval for it in both the immediate and wider family circles. Aunts, grandmothers and uncles all have something to say — usually negative. They will find the child badly brought up, badly groomed and so on. Everybody has something to recommend. Suggestions pour in. They even begin to interfere in its upbringing. All these know-it-alls should be locked out if the child is to be given a chance to develop without restraint.

A child's affections and dislikes cannot be controlled. There is practically no family — I mean family in its extended sense — in which there are not members who invite its anger and antagonism. But if you expect a small child to suppress its feelings and publicly exhibit the exactly opposite reactions, you are educating it to be insincere, and this emotion will re-appear throughout its life.

Life teaches early on - without any help from adults - that free reign cannot always be given to feelings. You should not suppress the unrestrained feelings of a small child which has not yet learned to react with indoctrinated common sense if you do not want to stifle it forever.

I said "indoctrinated" common sense because a child's behaviour does not lack true sense, but it is often not expedient and embarrasses parents.

Therefore it is much wiser to keep the family circle as small as possible and to adopt the point of view that the wider circle of relations in no way obliges you to account to it for the way your children are brought up or your ideas for a harmonious family life.

I mentioned that family life results from the concept embodying procreation. But this does not mean that marriage and family have automatically to be incorporated into a person's blueprint for life.

If his programme is based on another aspect, his interpretation of the meaning of his life is not incorrect. But he may not avoid starting a family only because he is afraid that he will not be able to use his finances for himself alone or because he will be obliged to renounce a comfortable and pleasure-filled existence.

Tomorrow we will discuss other programmes to underline that there may be differences in peoples' attitude to life.

Marriage and family not always necessary for the fulfilment of the blueprint.

YESTERDAY we spoke about people whose philosophy of life included the duty of parenthood and who, in fulfilment of this important task, should know which course to adopt and what to advise their children.

Now let us consider those who do not take the route of marriage and do not wish to have children.

This can be considered from various angles and is subject to many errors.

In the same way that marriage and parenthood are not always undertaken with noble thoughts and intentions but are often the result of coercion, so it is the other way around. A person predestined for marriage and mother- or fatherhood can be precluded from such a role by material influences. War, and its attendant miseries, often deflects the intended course.

But I do not want to discuss these exceptional circumstances, although, in the past decades they have occurred most frequently. I want to talk about programmes in which, right from the beginning,

MESSAGES FROM A DOCTOR IN THE FOURTH DIMENSION

people go through life alone, but nevertheless fulfil all the requirements for their present earthly existence.

In the case of quite extraordinary abilities in whatever field it may be justified - also from a material point of view - that a division of interests would obstruct or harm the development, creation or success. This is the case with great artists, whose correct marriage partner is somebody who supports and stimulates their unusual ability in an atmosphere of pure harmony and serene understanding.

But this is seldom the case. The result is usually an unsatisfactory marriage or diminished creative power. This is also why artists are called "easy-going" and "irresponsible." They seek the encouraging understanding of a good marriage in vain. You should actually be very cautious in your judgement of fellow men in matters which the individual personality alone has to account for as nobody can form an opinion about the next person without knowing him very well. You have only to consider how difficult it is to appraise yourself honestly and know yourself completely.

It must, of course, not be forgotten that the laws of civilisation prescribe certain types of behaviour that apply to everybody without exception as in view of existing conditions and — let us be honest — the prevailing immaturity of human beings there would be chaos and recklessness which would eclipse the sad enough state of their evolution.

But do not let us be too pessimistic! In this sphere too mistakes will lead to progress even though today's generation is not aware of it. What is lacking, as I have mentioned several times, is the necessary far-sightedness, the ability to assess matters in the proper perspective.

I hope that my suggestions will help people, who are uncertain about the rights and obligations that are their due, to find some indication that will free them from their doubts.

I have already mentioned that according to today's interpretation of the requirements for a perfectly accomplished life one has to prove oneself in three areas - marriage, friendship and career. The many failures show this theory to be incorrect. People may have the justifiable wish to marry, but this can undergo a change if, for some reason, the conditions are not suitable or the desired partner is not found. What matters now is how a person's attitude to life adapts to this precondition falling away.

According to today's teachings every unmarried person is a

being to be pitied and must consider himself a misfit who is inferior, incompetent and to be rejected by society. A sad condition for this earthly existence. And a completely wrong one.

A person to whom marriage is denied or who does not feel the wish for it in his innermost being should turn his attention to other matters. If he makes the effort, unimagined tasks will come his way. He will only be able to take on and achieve them if he is free in the material sense, which means without the obligation to maintain a family.

Unfortunately too few people know about these very important correlations, the reasons why they develop this way and their possibilities. But most important of all is that their outlook on life remains positive, even when a supposed failure or a necessary renunciation comes their way. The worst a person can do in such a case is resign himself to going to pieces and consider his life a failure and himself inferior and possibly underdeveloped.

Men as well as women are prone to this misconception. Considerably more consoling and encouraging literature on this subject should be offered than is now the case. How many positive energies are unused in this life and lost to the community instead of being harnessed for the benefit of the individual and the prosperity of mankind?

Disappointed young girls, deceived women and men unable to procreate have gone into monastries by the score in the past, for the most part only to disappear and avoid the supposed shame.

Gradually the realisation has dawned how mistaken this concept was and greater sexual freedom removes the feeling of shame and lessens the impact of malicious criticism.

But despite this new freedom and understanding that has made headway there are still people who torment themselves and consider their imaginary imperfection a disaster when they look at other people. They need sympathetic and correct instruction.

A doctor must not try to convince such a person that he has superior qualities in other directions in order to justify this supposed shortcoming. Everybody comes to earth with his complete blueprint. This is the only reason that he foregoes marriage and family.

But I have also pointed out that a woman who has already proved her motherly qualities in an earlier life can make use of them outside the family circle. She will do this automatically when the occasion arises.

In conclusion let me stress once again that nobody is of less value or less developed simply because his blueprint does not include marriage and children. May this comfort many a woman and as many men in their depressed state of mind and give them confidence in their outlook on life.

The search for life's blueprint is not the correct choice of a career. The end of life not synonymous with attaining one's goal.

YESTERDAY we talked of changes in life's plan and deemed them necessary, even obligatory if prerequisites for fulfilling the tasks stipulated in the blueprint fall away. Such changes can occur in all, or nearly all, basic concepts because it is by no means certain that what a person believes to have recognised as his programme is really so. Often the mistaken opinion prevails that it is the correct choice of a career and once this is mastered, life's task has been accomplished. So, to begin with, there must be a fundamental change in the interpretation of what the programme is before it can be applied.

Above all, there should not only be clarity about the links with the world beyond, but a programme to manage life's tasks should be searched for and set up. I will explain this once again so that there can be no misunderstanding.

Even people who do not believe in life after death must consider influences from the universe both possible and real as these are demonstrated quite clearly in research work done in natural science and technology. Incredulity may not lead to the denial of all values which must be cultivated for the promotion of a sense of community and a healthy life on this planet.

A confirmed materialist will probably not find true satisfaction in this existence, but he should not want to act obstructively or destructively. He too must have a sound opinion of life even though it may not be sound in all matters. Of course, his interpretation of the purpose of life will differ from that of somebody who sincerely believes in the true correlations in precisely those points which are of the greatest importance for the progress of mankind. These are the purely spiritual values which are given to people for the development of spirit and soul. For the materialist there is no calling in the true sense of the word, but only a career, an occupation, to maintain his existence and it must be as practical as possible.

A calling pre-supposes that a superior power "calls" a person, but a pure materialist would not acknowledge the existence of such an authority.

Nevertheless every effort must be made to convince just such people that higher powers than those on earth do exist. They must at least be shown the way that leads to progress even though they lack the comfort of belief and the goodwill.

Above all, the materialist who is of the opinion that possessions and power are life's supreme blessings will suffer much more with every setback than a person who is aware of the real values. Each disappointment will convince the materialist that his goals in life are severely reduced or totally lost.

The correct attitude to life is based on knowledge of the Eternal Almighty, recurring incarnation and the influences from the world beyond.

Of course, not everybody will avail himself of this clear and certain perception while on earth, but it is in his innermost being and will guide his thoughts and acts. Quite unconsciously, without any particular training he will reject a materialistic view of life. He will be satisfied with his lot or what his work brings him. This will always be the background of his emotional and spiritual development.

However, the environment could be a negative influence and suppress the positive fundamentals. This is why every opportunity should be used to teach people the correct fundamentals, build up their way of thinking and block out disturbing elements.

I consider this interpolation necessary because the different points of view cannot be mentioned often enough in order to present a clear picture of what I am trying to convey.

Man is endowed with powers of the spirit and body which allow him to organise his life at his discretion. His free will enables him to make use of these powers or let them atrophy. He can use them excessively or very sparingly. His understanding of their purpose will enable him to obtain the correct measure.

Therefore, in order to find the correct goal in life, which everybody has to do, it is imperative for him to know himself extremely well, be fully aware of his abilities, not live for the moment

MESSAGES FROM A DOCTOR IN THE FOURTH DIMENSION

and not let himself drift. Whoever does this is in great danger. He opens the door to all powers - not only the good ones - and becomes their plaything.

This is why it is most important to adapt yourself to the blueprint brought to earth. The ability to master it is available.

I have already mentioned that the powers of the spirit and body are given to a person to achieve his blueprint and he has to make use of them. We are going to examine them in broad outline and see to what extent they are necessary in order to develop a philosophy of life.

They are mainly expressed though free will, which is the basic platform. The will to think, to use his brain and to come to a logical conclusion indicates the path to be followed.

In addition, it is necessary for him to know his inherent powers and limitations as well as the possibilities that the environment offers.

Thinking and testing, feeling what is hidden within waiting to be awakened, is of prime importance. If his aims indicate high moral ideals and he has confidence in guidance from the other world, his inner, purely spiritual, power will point the way. The guiding thought must be to realise his tasks and obligations, not pursue a pointless, comfortable life without the willingness to make sacrifices.

For this he is given physical powers commensurate with his blueprint. He has to use them, ever mindful of the fact that a long life requires a healthy, efficient body.

No goal is short term. In fact, one lifetime only provides a small section of a far-reaching, on-going programme. This is why he should not assume that he will attain it in one earthly existence.

But now we have to discuss the nature of such goals so that what I am saying is understandable. It is not a goal to be materially measured and assessed.

The spiritual goal of a person must greatly exceed earthly existence. His endeavours only point him in the direction and - as I have already said - he will be happy if he is able to find his path. But along it there are stations, characterised by career and calling, suffering and happiness, riches and poverty, and the manner in which he deals with them.

It is a massive subject. Tomorrow we will continue.

Moral and legal obligation.

TODAY I want to introduce a new aspect of a positive attitude to life: understanding for other peoples' troubles. I don't wish to call it sympathy, rather it is your attitude towards the problems of your fellow men; in how far you pay attention to them or you are obliged to do so.

Some obligations can be considered moral and others, legal.

Moral obligations originate in your conscience, your personal spiritual domain and are not affected by external influences. Legal obligations are determined by civilisation, by regulations within the state or nation. In no way can they be compared with moral ones. Morality implies decency and places kindliness or selflessness above everything. You cannot avoid a moral obligation because it only occurs when your personal interpretation of right conduct bids you to behave in a certain manner.

An example will illustrate what I mean. A person is in trouble and, apart from a good, true friend, has no one to turn to. He comes to his friend, not to ask for charity, but the friend has already sized up the situation and gives him what he needs. There is no legal obligation in this case because there are no family connections or other bonds. Help is offered purely on a basis of sensitivity - the feeling conveyed from the soul to the spirit entity.

Take another example. A person falls in the street and breaks a leg. No kind passer-by witnessing the accident would leave the scene without rendering aid, no matter in how much of a hurry he happened to be. The picture of helplessness that flashes past his inner eye causes him to forget all personal interests because morally, as a decent person, he feels himself obliged to help.

But a person is not always subject to an ethical responsibility in this sense. Very often he only acts in this way because he fears to appear contemptible, make a bad impression on others, lose face and so on.

A moral obligation is only fulfilled when an act comes from a pure heart without thoughts of personal gain or the wish to make oneself respected. One often hears a person say, "I had to do it because I am more or less morally obliged." Such acts are based on thoughts that certainly are far removed from morality, but have come about due to some compulsion which has not been prompted by law.

Many legal obligations would not have to be defined as such, because they are motivated by moral considerations. The reason they are declared legal is because people who are entitled to claim the fulfilment of such obligations are put into the position of enforcing their right with outside help. This explains the term. I will elaborate further.

A positive attitude to life encompasses the knowledge that you must not only think of your own interests. Everybody has a moral obligation to his fellow men, the environment and, in fact, the whole of humanity. Whoever thinks that he is not bound to this constraint, violates nature's laws as well as the rules prescribed by custom. It is a fraction of all-embracing love, a tiny step closer to truth if one consciously does justice to these dictates and does not shirk the obligations which occur daily, even hourly, in social life.

The concept "consideration" is part of this. It signifies a moral attitude towards the environment, one which stems solely from sentiment. It means that you feel yourself committed, without legal pressure, without thoughts of personal gain. You must only check, that your actions do not hamper or disturb others. This, not only in tangible and visible social relations, but also in thinking and speaking, in every form of contact with other people.

As we have used the word "moral" let us reflect on its meaning for a moment. A sound philosophy of life requires the correct assessment of morality. Actually, I don't need to enlarge on the subject if I consider that the goal of everybody on earth is a striving towards all-embracing love. Nevertheless, it is not easy to understand the notion of all-embracing love and build your life on it if we do not take into consideration the individual areas in which it has to hold good.

There is much talk about morality, but seldom is it properly explained. It is not difficult to do so. The quality of being moral implies the clear understanding of the correlations of the spiritual, physical, emotional and intellectual aspects of civilisation, therefore, of social relations. Morality is not a word that the individual can apply to himself, but only to his relationship with other people.

The relationship between "you" and "I," between "I" and "you" makes it possible to define morality.

The degree of moral conduct is evident in your attitude towards your partner and your combined attitude towards other people.

The standard of moral conduct can be greater or lesser. There can be doubts as to its limits. Its total rejection can be termed immoral.

Every extreme conduct which violates custom and law, causes disgust and damages health, must be considered immoral. But people tend to limit its use to the sexual relationship between men and women.

According to the same ethical principles, fraud, robbery and all crimes contrary to law that intentionally inflict damage to life and limb and the property of another are deemed immoral. Seen from a higher standpoint the basis is much the same. Abuse of a human body is as much a crime as robbery, even though the partner consents. People must learn that with every infringement energy can be wasted, feelings hurt and health damaged.

Morality is not developed to the same degree in everybody and is not equally understood by everybody. What one person finds quite normal and ethically correct, another will consider a grievous infringement which causes the most extreme emotional stress.

Morality is not a clear cut norm that can be summed up in a few words. Everybody's individual point of view will cause him to define it according to his inherent spiritual and emotional maturity. But in general one can say that a person who lives according to nature and observes the manners and customs of those around him with a sense of propriety can be considered ethically mature.

The various interpretations of morality could generate a great deal of work. For our studies we'll leave it at that. I only want to induce you to think about what I have said, define your limits clearly and realise that you have perhaps made mistakes from which you have to learn.

Poverty and wealth as bases for the achievement of life's tasks.

TODAY I will continue to supplement the list of fundamentals necessary for a positive attitude to life in order to widen the scope of our thoughts. We have, of course, pointed out several times that the assessment of matter and its utilisation in the right measure is an important aspect, but within the structure of our discussion it is necessary to add a few more ideas.

Just as the maturity and intellect of one person can differ radically from another so too does the utilisation and enjoyment of material goods. A person born into a wealthy environment has, at first, no occasion to consider the uneven distribution of affluence and will only learn later to compare his background with that of other people. But a child born into circumstances of misery and privation will begin to wonder much sooner why his lot is less fortunate. Civilisation, which has attained a standard level of development, should not know misery and privation. There should not be such an unbridgeable gap between the two extremes.

But as I have already said, it is not important whether somebody is blessed with more material goods and property than the next person; it only matters that everybody has sufficient for his earthly existence in order to meet the demands of his blueprint.

A person who makes it his duty to prove his community sense by serving and helping and renounces material advantages to do so will be content to possess only as much as he needs to maintain his existence. Another, who has taken it upon himself to look after others, in the material sense, in order to do justice to social requirements, will need a broader financial basis if he wants to do more than just construct social institutions and train assistants.

Wealth, even if it belongs to an individual, must bear interest in some way for the community. It must be to its advantage. It must serve it. As we see it from here, every wealthy man is not only the sole owner, but also the administrator and caretaker of material assets which are given to him by Divine Omnipotence and come with considerable obligations.

The possessions of this world do not fall into anybody's lap without a definite purpose and mission. If it is only as much as he can use for himself and his family, it is good to know that moderation and reserve alone ensure the fulfilment of spiritual tasks intended for incarnate life.

Wealth, therefore, always implies more, or less, responsibility. The degree depends on the amount and its fundamental worth.

On the one hand, those blessed with prosperity should become increasingly aware of this irrefutable truth. They should consider an equitable participation for those who need more means and possibilities than their environment offers to establish suitable conditions for the community as stipulated in their blueprints.

You could argue that this distribution should have taken place at the outset if incarnation occurs according to the criteria of the blueprint. This is certainly correct and in future will be the case. But for the time being people are so mistaken about the value of material possessions that scarcely one is prepared to relinquish even a small portion of what he has inherited or worked for. But eventually people will have to realise that their intrinsic worth and progress in no way depends on the size of their fortune.

On the other hand, people in modest circustances - and by modest I don't mean those in extreme cases who, in contrast to the wealthy, live in abject poverty - must learn to understand that their happiness and contentment would not be any greater if they had more possessions. This is an aspect of a positive philosophy of life. As I have already mentioned, the incorrect assessment of the value of matter is the main cause of so much emotional suffering and such constant failure in the battle for existence.

Of course, it is easy for me to preach. I am free of the burden of matter. I am merely absorbing spiritual values and can only pass these on.

But I can see that the distribution of material possessions is according to the infinite laws of the universe even though mankind considers it unjust. People lack the good will and wisdom to recognise the individual's proper and adequate limits.

But you have to be able to distinguish between the assets and possessions reserved for an individual's enjoyment and those which are earmarked for the community, even if a single person is their owner. This does not mean that other people have the right to control such assets and possessions. Their purpose is that they be used. This is often far more satisfying and enjoyable for those who do not bear the responsibility for their maintenance and administration than it is for their rightful proprietor.

Owners of large fortunes, who were spiritually very advanced and knew that many people depended on them for their livelihood, considered this matter and increased the value of their holdings through just and humane administration.

Many generations of such families with an advanced philosophy of life served the cause of social development, but war, hatred, envy and greed have destroyed much of it again.

With this brief message about the value of material possessions, their wise utilisation and the avoidance of an excess, I wish to make people think whether, for this existence on earth they are sufficiently, amply or over-endowed. Everybody can easily establish what he could have done without or what actually is a burden.

Of course, this means he has to be totally honest with himself. A person will always have desires and think he cannot live without a certain possession. But occasionally he may come to the opposite conclusion and eventually might actually be happy to have renounced it. The more difficult it is to obtain something, the more useless it turns out to be once it has been acquired.

Learn to listen more to your inner voice, your conscience. Ask your good guide what is really desirable. Don't allow yourself to be influenced by show and external appearances.

The fear of poverty, which only afflicts those who have too many possessions, is to be totally condemned. They well know how easily material riches vanish if they are not properly administered or if war and persecution stretch out their claws.

The obsession of poverty is the penalty, I would say, for greed, but if one wants a quiet existence, it ought to be the signal for the worthlessness of material possessions.

I think I have said enough about this subject today and close with the wish that many a good, but possession-loving person will be motivated to alter his life-style.

The possibility of making good a programme that has gone wrong. Sound and abnormal imagination. Spiritualism is not a game.

TODAY I want to describe how a spirit entity, who in earthly existence was not able to discover the right path in life, finds it in the world beyond and can link up with his past existence. It is a difficult ordeal and necessitates extensive self-criticism and a great deal of willingness.

A spirit entity who has already attained a certain maturity and higher stage of development in past lives will soon be aware of his faults and wish himself back in the material world where he would be able to re-trace his steps and find the correct course. It is the same desire that many people on earth have when it becomes obvious that they could have made a greater success of this or that undertaking.

How often one hears: "If I come back to earth, I'm going to handle things differently — or better. I wouldn't like to be so clumsy and ignorant again. My life would have been different if I had had the experience of old age in my youth." Many think and speak in this way and seem very earnest. But in the main people make these statements jokingly. It is a miracle if one person in a thousand really means what he says. It is considered pure imagination when he speaks of returning and repeating. But it can safely be taken seriously because imagination is also a phenomenon that people on earth cannot fully understand or explain.

One speaks of a sound or abnormal imagination, depending on whether the subject in question is intelligible according to earthly concepts. It is not always possible to understand imagination because it is the reflection of ideas which have been gathered during life in the world beyond. They are embodied in the spirit entity and transferred in accordance with the ability to assimilate them in the present incarnate life.

Everything man cannot explain in common sense terms is considered abnormal, even crazy. Some of these impressions are detrimental in so far as they actually derive from the influence of inferior spirit entities. The exploration of this occurrence is an important step in the treatment of mentally disturbed individuals. Doctors should study it very seriously. Best results depend on profound belief and total conviction in the links between this world and the next.

Already now I can see that it will not be long before leading scientists overcome their reserve and discuss these matters quite openly.

Spiritualism is no game for sensation-seekers or those trying to gain material advantages from it. It is, I would say, a religious act which has nothing to do with rosaries and babbling prayers but is simply religion in an all-embracing sense, in its union with the cosmos and its positive energies.

I am not merely stringing words together. This is extremely profound knowledge which will only benefit those in the true sense of the word who fully accept what I say, act accordingly and thereby serve humanity.

So a person who has followed the wrong path in life, either

because of selfishness and the worship of material possessions or because of an obstruction caused by the environment and custom, realises, when he enters the world beyond, that he has, in no way, or at least not in the most essential aspects, fulfilled his programme. In accordance with the maturity he has achieved, his errors will most probably not exceed those of previous lifetimes. They are measured according to the infinite laws and, as I have already pointed out, there is no judgement. Everybody forms his own opinion regarding the extent of his progress or his lack of development. His free will has to decide whether he should be satisfied with the result of his earthly existence and can take a rest or whether he has to do something in order not to be left behind by his companions.

I have already mentioned that everybody carries deep inside him the urge to progress which he cannot resist, but which can be masked and repressed by ignoring the purpose of life and the necessity of serving humanity. It may be a comfort for people who feel they have not fulfilled their tasks and erred in many ways to know that they can make good what they neglected to do even if, when they return to earth again, they remember nothing and cannot automatically begin to build on particular fundamentals.

You can believe me when I say that with each return to earth the power of the soul grows. Furthermore, the opportunity to make good in the world beyond is always available so that the following existence on earth will make for greater progress. Let us avoid the illusion that incarnate life represents the zenith of our existence. It is and remains an extremely low rung of the ladder. However brightly our personality sparkles according to earthly standards, modesty must be the main basis on which we must build further for it alone enables our sights to be set on higher values.

Modesty is not synonymous with a low opinion of yourself. Once again, the middle course is the ideal solution. What has been achieved and what good deeds have been accomplished for your fellow men should duly be recognised and appreciated. But never allow it to become arrogance. This is so easily the case in medicine. Here particularly the greatest failures occur and the greatest damage caused.

Let us consider how people can find the correct path without knowing the programme they have brought with them to life on earth.

Everybody can test himself and discover his capabilities. For this he does not have to consult specialists and be examined as is often the case today.

It is not difficult to establish a self-portrait. It only requires a certain method according to which everybody can analyse his own behaviour and see how and when he can apply his abilities. But to do this, he must be totally honest with himself. He must be guided how to discover correct opinions and convictions in order to picture himself faithfully without mincing matters.

We have put together a set of guidelines to help those who are searching for the right path.

When a person is young he can often be stimulated to compare his own ideas with those of other people who have distinguished themselves in various ways. This is a kind of subconscious self-analysis. To study examples is important. They generally point the way and will always do so. Just as children copy the behaviour of adults, so adults imitate their role models. They must, of course, be the right role models, not people who have gained an undeserved reputation through clever publicity and perhaps the incorrect use of material values and possessions.

Today we stop here. Tomorrow we will outline the guidelines necessary to establish this valuable self-portrait.

Some basic rules for those seeking progress and truth.
The boundaries between egotism and altruism.

YESTERDAY I spoke about a complete programme and how a person should be trained to identify and build his life around it in order to fulfil his tasks.

Now let us set down some basic rules which will signpost the way for those seeking progress and truth.

Once again I remind you that these rules are not for people who still regard material possessions as life's most desirable goal and take it for granted that they live only once.

Begin by finding a role model with exceptional characteristics and spiritual qualities.

To achieve spiritual progress it is necessary to know which of these characteristics have to be fully developed, which suppressed and which have to be cultivated as a basis for a worthy vocation.

The most important principle is to serve mankind altruistically; this leaves no place for egotism. But altruism may not lead to self-renunciation, because without a healthy measure of self-respect no one can make progress in life.

From childhood this basic attitude to your own personality must be awakened and the limits observed so that you do not succumb to arrogance and conceit.

Self-respect implies modesty and consideration for the people around, especially when a highly developed spirit entity grows up amongst those who are his inferiors and are forced to look up to him. These are not opinions based on profound reflections. Rather, it is knowledge gathered during earlier lives and filed away in the soul.

Now, according to the logical laws of nature these sequels are transmitted from the soul to the mind. Already in earliest childhood there is an astonishing degree of superiority towards adults who cannot establish the reason. In some cases the intellectually inferior person will attempt to dominate the more highly developed child because he wishes to call the tune. Another will try to remain indifferent so as not to have to acknowledge the child's predominance, but it is seldom the case that an adult fully acknowledges its pre-eminence and takes pains to promote its self-confidence which is on a par with its superiority.

This differentiation is vital. It is of the utmost importance to set guidelines for fair judgement. In fact, such guidelines should first be given to those adults who still wrongly consider themselves superior simply because they are the creators of the body and psyche of their children.

Where then are the boundaries of altruism and egotism? When is an egotistical attitude permissible? When must it be suppressed?

Egotism is always allowed and necessary if the preservation of life is at stake, if the personality has to be cared for, if intellectual standards have to be furthered and goals, which fulfil a calling and are based on particular values, have to be pursued. In such matters there dare not be renunciation even if people around make other demands and try to force a course upon you that is way below your spiritual level when you not only seem predestined for higher things but also feel it.

To neglect your own personality, which means to ignore your abilities because the opposite course is more convenient and involves less work, is a mistake which will have harmful results and bring your spiritual development to a full stop. The pretext of wanting to serve humanity with comfortable tasks which require no particular talent is by no means altruism. On the contrary, it is egotism and lacks responsibility. Of course, people are easily inclined to label such work a sacrifice or devotion because they have no way of establishing in how far the person's capabilities exceed the simple efforts he is making.

Nobody is really incapable of knowing, deep within himself, whether he has chosen the right course and used his spiritual maturity to the full. Often outward appearances mean more to him than inner satisfaction. In the final analysis, he is convinced that the opinion of his fellow men justifies his attitude.

It is not easy for the individual to lead an altruistic life consciously and deliberately for the benefit of mankind. Such absolute dedication cannot be demanded or too literally interpreted because matter claims its rights and as the basis of earthly existence it cannot be ignored. Once again it is a case of a harmonious balance, characterised by the command, "Love your neighbour as yourself." This concept guides you to apply your energies for your fellow men as much as you do for yourself and extend the good thoughts you have for your own person to others. The power of thought generates a positive approach to life if it is guided by high moral ideals and it works inwardly as well as outwardly.

This is the correct way to establish a balance between yourself and your surroundings; a balance based on clear-cut considerations and good intentions.

This is why parents should never demand that a child is dominated by its siblings just because it is too compliant and doesn't have the strength to fight for its place in the sun.

Of course a programme brought to earth often includes being of service to cleanse the effects of mistakes made in past lives. But such a purification and consequent karmic liberation is only possible if every burden is accepted with a pure heart and without reluctance and inner resistance.

Altruism in the truest sense of the word is to consider the next person without self-interest, to perform a good deed, to make a sacrifice without thinking of yourself. A mother is able to do this. She becomes a role model for her children and her husband, who is often quite ashamed to admit that he is hardly in a position for self-sacrifice. Motherhood is therefore the purest example of altruism. If it did not exist, the worlds would die out, for they would be devoid of new blood. This is our point of view from our more advanced standpoint.

I think I have explained the first principle for establishing the programme for life in sufficient detail, although I could enlarge on the subject. But I prefer to allow you some leeway to consider what I have written about without over-complication. Nevertheless, we will return to these ideas over and over again until the pattern begins to fall into place and take shape.

Spiritual values are never lost. The difference between "goodness" and "kindness"

A POSITIVE attitude to life obliges everybody to fulfil tasks and take on responsibilities. They differ from person to person, both in composition and the degree of difficulty. This is why it is essential to bear in mind that everybody cannot be equally endowed with material possessions and that there are other values which have to be cultivated.

People who correctly interpret the deeper purpose of life will instinctively search out their tasks and judge how to go about them. They will consider which of the elements they have incarnated with will be of use in this work; these are essentials which they have already acquired in previous incarnations.

It is never too late to attend to tasks because realisation often dawns later in life when a person has learned to know himself and judge what in the course of years has contributed to his spiritual progress and what has held him back.

If you consider how few people are aware of the correlations which I keep referring to in my messages, it is relatively simple to imagine what immense progress the next generation would make if people on earth today would make use of the information I am passing on and include it in the education of their children so that it serves as a foundation for the future.

We have discussed egotism and altruism as the corner stones of a correct philosophy of life. Let us assume that a person has recognised the ideal equilibrium between these two characteristics and really tries to incorporate this harmonious balance into his life. It should not be difficult for him to do so because a good intention always reaches its goal. It is not a matter of battling for material possessions but for spiritual values. Nobody can dispute his right to these. Here we have the crux of the matter. Everything of this nature to be achieved is within man. If he seeks a spiritually advanced life, the groundwork must be firmly entrenched in his soul and spirit.

Whoever knows the first principles of a correct attitude to life but does nothing to achieve them has not yet matured spiritually to a point where he feels that the striving for truth and progress is his most important obligation. He blames his failure either on the people around him or unfavourable circumstances which leave him no time to pay attention to himself and so on. A person like this still has lesser tasks to fulfil, but this does not preclude him from making progress — however limited — in spiritual spheres.

The concept of altruism which we have defined in its purest sense also has distinctive qualities which can be practised to a lesser or greater degree. These are "goodness" and "kindness."

I have already mentioned that the word "goodness" can be applied to a selfless act without personal benefit. This is dedication in the spiritual as well as the material sense and in its most extreme form can be termed a sacrifice.

Kindness is more than affection, but does not go so far as to sacrifice material possessions. It is understanding, forgiveness and compassion for a fellow man who turns to his neighbour for help and advice because the latter's manner seems to hold the promise of fulfilling his wishes or desires.

Goodness is therefore an important element in the ground rules that I want you to be aware of, because it leads to the inner peace, harmony and spiritual maturity which is needed to fulfil the life programme.

One cannot be good with logical determination. It is an attribute anchored in the personality. Whoever lacks it must be trained to resist opposite sentiments and study himself critically in order to emulate those who as good role-models show him the correct way to behave.

I mentioned spiritual maturity and harmony as qualities needed to establish the programme for life. Only he who is able to tune in to his innermost being and is guided by his soul has the good fortune to see clearly where his path lies.

But we must make a clear distinction between the demands of material life — the preservation of bodily existence — and the more important demands of the spirit entity who wishes to advance to a level in the fourth dimension higher than the one it previously occupied. No power on earth can stifle this innermost desire. Wars are only waged for material ends. They will cease when people realise how unwarranted and useless this struggle for might and possession is and that spiritual progress will never be achieved in this way. The battles in the name of the Church in the past are to be condemned as much as the wars and fighting between nations today.

Power does not imply justice and only infringes the basic principles of all-embracing love which alone can give mankind peace and spiritual freedom. It may occur to you that this goal is unimaginably far away. Yes, with incarnate sight this is so, but from our more advanced point of view we see a positive development. Time means nothing to us and does not have to be taken into consideration.

Do not imagine that within the timespan of a few generations it is possible to achieve the ideal that I have portrayed. With great patience, much forbearance and goodwill a tiny step forward can be taken each lifetime.

Do not lose courage. The only way is forward and upward. The belief in hell and damnation is a concept of incarnate life; it imposes ordeals that are misleading and generally very hard to master.

Try to convince people to test and train themselves, and help them to recognise the tasks that everyone has to perform in the service of others.

Tomorrow we will continue to investigate the various inferences of goodness because it is important to formulate the distinction clearly and underline the various meanings.

The purpose of eternal laws is spiritual perfection. "Evil" as opposed to "goodness." The development of mankind as seen from the other world.

GOODNESS and kindness are words that are used very often, but not necessarily in the correct context because no consideration is given to their meaning.

People who are good usually go unnoticed because they are

quiet, do not flaunt this important quality and are reluctant to believe that it can actually be attributed to them. Just as a wise man constantly bears in mind how little he really knows, so the genuinely good person is never wholly convinced that he has already attained the highest degree of this virtue.

Only careful thought will make these subtle differences clear. They are subtle only by incarnate standards, not by those of the fourth dimension. But peoples' reflection are important and should be cultivated. Their insight ought to be improved to enable them to make correct judgements.

There is a subtle difference between the meaning of the word knowledge and the word wisdom. The same applies to goodness and kindness, whereas knowledge is not to be interpreted as being a lesser degree of wisdom or kindness of goodness. I draw your attention to this because people very often use these words incorrectly. For instance, you say to a friend from whom you want a favour, "Be so good..." without really meaning good in the true sense of the word. To do somebody a favour can be termed kind, but only if it is performed with a feeling of wanting to oblige the other person and there is no self-interest. I explain these concepts so minutely so that you really learn to study yourself correctly and decide to act accordingly.

There are many mistakes that have to be rectified, both in the positive and negative sense. Negative, because many people have a low opinion of their own conduct and then suffer from an inferiority complex which is not justified.

We have said that the life-programme has to be established. It is not necessary to seek out the tasks that allow this programme to be fulfilled. They have been prepared for everybody and will be brought to him. He has only to accept them and dedicate himself to them body and soul, as the saying goes. Nobody need fear that he will be overlooked and excluded from Divine Omnipotence and the immutable laws. If he is tuned in, he will find his way to them and be able to handle them.

For nobody is assigned tasks that are too difficult to master. But I must also stress that there is a difference between tasks in the purely material sense and those allotted to the spirit and soul. I see only the latter from here as I am not burdened with material problems. But we will discuss these as well as they have to be solved so that the spirit and soul can progress without restriction.

We have not yet talked about the opposite of goodness. The word "evil" is often used in the wrong sense. Evil is only that which contravenes the eternal laws and deliberately works against them. Ignorance of these laws is a sign of a very low level of development. Those whose knowledge is more advanced should help to raise the standard.

Really evil people are much less in evidence than those who are backward and ignorant.

From our more advanced point of view in the discarnate world we can see that progress is being made but, as I have said, this is not apparent from one generation to the next. The process is not like an operation where an organ is removed and perhaps replaced by another one. In the same way that emotional suffering can dominate the greater part of a human life and can only be countered by patience, so the progress of mankind must be seen in relation to the entire spiritual kingdom's gradual approach to perfection. It must reach this goal because it is the purpose of the eternal laws.

But to revert to evil, I must stress that a person who is striving to find the truth and to know and better himself can in no way be evil. A deed may be evil in the human sense, but the perpetrator need not be so.

When I began these messages, I mentioned that the concepts of good and evil are different in the incarnate and discarnate spheres. Now I will make this difference clear.

Cause and effect have often to be judged from quite opposing points of view. An evil deed - by human standards a crime - can stem from a cause that leads, quite understandably, to an evil act without necessarily having emanated from evil thoughts and intentions. This applies to acts committed in the heat of passion which cause the guilty person deep remorse even though he does not admit it and attempts to justify his behaviour.

It is barely possible to understand the thought process of a person who commits a crime. The reaction called forth by the resulting consequences means very little because in the main it arises from logical reflection. The emotional implications are seldom obvious. But they alone can confirm whether a criminal is really evil and one would have to look into his soul to do so. This is why people often make mistakes in their judgement which is understandable if everything not in accordance with incarnate law is labelled evil. Under these circumstances, it is no wonder that the global situation of mankind is depicted so negatively and people are filled with hopelessness instead of confidence.

Nevertheless I do not intend to gloss over the obstacles that hinder the material progress of life and cause fear, hardship and uncertainty.

Rest assured that evil does not predominate. Mistakes are made, but they can be rectified. With good will they can be controlled.

I have already mentioned that goodness is not as readily recognisable as evil and this leads to incorrect conclusions. The process of development needs great courage and faith to overcome the obstacles placed across your path.

This is why I want to introduce a new concept which will help you to master your life programme.

Meet your tasks head-on with courage. There must be no hesitant side-stepping in the belief that you do not have the necessary ability to take them on. Once you begin working at them your abilities will increase; if necessary, beyond all bounds. There are many good examples of this. For instance, artists with a calling occasionally produce outstanding work in a way no other person could. I have already pointed out that help comes from the cosmos to everybody and, I would add, falls into the lap of whoever strides confidentally and trustingly along the path that he has recognised as the one designated for him.

A calling is a divine gift and a mark of distinction. It places an obligation on the recipient and demands more energy and emotional commitment than mere professional activity. The scope of such a person is extensive and knows no material bounds. This is the big difference between a career and a calling, which I have already spoken about. With this I close for today. Tomorrow I will discuss new ideas that are important for the establishment and mastery of the life programme.

MESSAGES FROM A DOCTOR IN THE FOURTH DIMENSION

The perfect human being does not exist. The lie is an attribute of civilisation. Spiritual work depends on the physical disposition.

WE have discussed several qualities which provide the basis for realising the blueprint brought to earth. If we examine them, we find that without exception they are characteristics which determine the contemporary personality. In many hundred or even thousand years there will be other norms required in a person's character.

People embody these virtues in varying degrees but nobody does so to perfection. A person in a condition of complete excellence does not exist.

Our spiritual circle only puts forward the name of one personality from the past who attained this state of grace and whose teachings we can understand. Jesus Christ. This in itself will serve to convince you how far removed man today is from the standards of the Messiah.

Nevertheless the goal must remain as an incentive, and the aspirant begin by being completely honest with himself about his shortcomings and what is hampering his soul so that it is not performing as it should or whether his spirit is transmitting the impulse of will. Honesty with himself and with others is one of the main requirements in judging achievements and the importance of thoughts and actions. The highest standards need not be attained immediately, but the ways and means to do so must be sought.

It is not easy to be honest with yourself. Many a person thinks he is, but invariably he is being insincere in order not to have to reproach himself or, on the other hand, because he loves his mistakes and takes pleasure in cultivating them.

But whoever wants to follow the path that has been suggested will not go far if he builds his life on lies and deceit. This may cause indignant reproach and the accusation that I am malevolent and cannot find a good word to say for anybody, but I must tell you, I can look into your souls and see how few of you try to be truthful and avoid deceitful thoughts and remarks.

Often it is the people around you who expect or demand a specific way of thinking and force you to conceal your real feelings so that you become extremely reserved or actually lie in order not to cause confusion or anger.

In many matters civilisation demands adaption to the rules of conduct established and enforced by authority and custom and forbids truth to come into its own. It is not necessary to furnish examples of this. Everyone knows what I mean. Once the varying degrees of spiritual development have been brought to a common level and the differing opinions on the purpose of life are balanced throughout human society, lies will belong to the past and people will come together open-heartedly, embracing truth.

Let us imagine that the world is free of lies and everything we encounter can be taken at face value. Joy would know no bounds! As inconceivable as this state of affairs is today, it nevertheless highlights what tasks everybody still has to accomplish so that this ideal condition can come about.

All the qualities that have to be developed are spiritual. Life on earth offers this opportunity. Progress is in direct relation to the strength of the soul. This is why attention must be paid to all the primary principles that affect both it and the spirit.

By this I do not mean to imply that we have discussed all the virtues of purely emotional and mental origin. I only want to extend the subject into the material field to avoid being too one-sided.

When I compare the capabilities of the soul and spirit in the fourth dimension I see how cramped and hampered they are in the rough shell that the body offers. But for incarnate man this is the natural condition.

I need not dwell on the importance of the body's function. That its care must go hand in hand with the welfare of the soul and the demands of the spirit is obvious because the spirit entity makes its will known through the brain. Of course, the nervous system has to absorb the stimulus of the soul in order to transmit it to the spirit entity and the organs.

I was a neurologist on earth and obtained considerable experience in this field. A lot of it was correct and of some value, but the rest was less than perfect and completely wrong. Though it was not contrary to the accepted scientific teaching at the time, today I can see that this teaching has to be corrected and supplemented. This is not only in relation to psychic problems and matters which concern the behaviour of people — about which individual psychology still has a lot to learn — but also in respect of a complex of matters concerning organ neurology as well as individual issues. Up to now these have not been solved because doctors have been working in a mistaken direction.

MESSAGES FROM A DOCTOR IN THE FOURTH DIMENSION

This will be a part of the work that I will present to my medical colleagues but it is not suitable for these messages.

I don't think I need to list the necessities for the correct care and physical training of the body. In a nutshell it is moderation in all things, particularly in food and drink as well as an orderly way of life. Technical achievements have offered people an easier life. But technology has also caused the body considerable damage through stress. Great attention must be paid to countering this or it will affect the spirit and soul.

Excessive stress, which can also be caused by noise and pollution, irritates the soul and prevents it from carrying out its work properly. Then the organs do not function to the extent they should. An irregular pattern begins to emerge, damaging the entire system. The reaction on the soul is a decrease in vital energy, causing spiritual activity to be handicapped. You can study this problem from whichever aspect you choose but all the sections are interdependent so one cannot function without the others.

When working on the life programme it is necessary to keep checking whether the components are functioning together in a well-balanced manner. By components I mean soul, spirit and body. Fortitude and energy do not flow from a sick, weak body. Strenuous efforts have to be made to overcome a lack of physical energy.

Physical energy is not to be regarded as something that is produced by an above-average constitution to accomplish extraordinary bodily achievements. Rather it is the standard physical condition which a regular, natural life style gives everybody who is healthy and has had a normal birth and upbringing.

People who have suffered external influences like improper nourishment and attention will have to find a totally different programme to follow. If they pay more than average attention to spiritual progress, they will find their development will outstrip that of people with their full physical powers.

What I have mentioned briefly in this chapter is an indication - and only an indication - as to how to find and realise the blueprint for life. It must not be interpreted as being the complete description of all the inter-relationships in the human organism. Everybody who has read to this point will have questions to ask. I still have many things to explain. But enough for today.

Prominent qualities indicate the blueprint.
What has been mastered cannot be lost.

YESTERDAY we spoke about how people have to study and test themselves, decide which character traits to develop and how to work at perfecting them in this incarnation. They must appraise the cause of their weaknesses in order to analyse them critically and honestly to the best of their ability. We have already discussed the principal virtues which must be particularly considered and exploited.

If I say nothing new because these concepts are sufficiently well known and their relative worth is obvious, I am nevertheless compelled to mention them because they are linked to the search for life's blueprint.

If we think about it, these values constitute a general blueprint and are a part of everybody's life, but they are seldom developed to the same degree. Therefore, it is necessary to investigate where leverage must be applied.

But quite apart from this purely personal task, one fundamental quality is present in practically every person. This is a tendency, an ability, a gift in a certain direction which enables him to make his mark in life. This particular, dominating attribute which makes him what he is, indicates the tasks he has to fulfil — his life programme. Should he make a mistake and not understand what this task is, it by no means signifies a delay in his progress. But it can cause disappointments and difficulties which require more emotional and mental stamina to overcome than would have been necessary if he had correctly assessed his life's course.

Free will is always the deciding factor. Some influences may detract from his decision to keep to his purpose of life but whatever has already been developed and mastered with good will is permanently preserved.

For instance, a person who feels he has the calling to be a teacher in order to help others to succeed must, above all, have a great deal of patience. If he lacks this, he will soon realise that he is not making progress, that he is causing resistance in his pupils and his soul does not make the necessary contact with his work should it really be a vocation. But this does not mean that he must resign himself to failure, admit his inadequacy and conclude that he has chosen the wrong career. He can make up the qualities he lacks in a short time once he musters the good will to do so.

It is the same with the medical profession as I have mentioned often enough. Doctors should undergo a thorough self-examination to check how many of the qualities they need, they actually have. Third persons or patients cannot make such an assessment, and if they do, it is too late. The ethical fundamentals which medical students are taught should be firmly rooted in their soul and spirit if they want to be true helpers of mankind.

There is a big difference between service to other people being offered within a family or to strangers.

A natural bond exists within the family circle even though a true harmony of souls is seldom apparent. It is much more difficult to establish this link with outsiders who must first be won over and usually conceal their need for help.

It is far easier for a mother to feel the needs of her children but she must want to do this. She must not overlook this important task should she be caught up in material matters.

Service to other people not only implies a feeling for their needs but also empathy and sympathetic understanding for their problems.

Actually we shouldn't even have to discuss such matters. But mankind has not yet reached the stage of maturity where it can afford to ignore instruction.

People tend to live only for the moment and at the end of a busy day instead of satisfaction they usually experience an inner void. This is because their day did not include consideration, or even the thought of it, for other people.

Everybody can do one small, good deed a day, even if it is only a friendly word or a heartfelt "thank you" for help and encouragement offered. And this even though the daily grind offers little leeway for more important achievements.

An individual should experience his own reaction when he proffers a friendly greeting. His dismal thoughts are banished and he becomes cheerful. Encouraged by his own happy reaction he should make a deliberate effort to continue in this way.

I want particularly to stress once again that nobody should become discouraged if he thinks he has not properly identified his programme. Life is long enough for it to become obvious at the proper time. The very fact that he is on the lookout for it shows great progress because he gets to know his own character and recognises its shortcomings which he must eliminate. It is a personal victory and makes him happy to know that he has examined himself with brutal frankness and overcome his mistakes.

I mentioned that life is long enough to identify the programme in good time. But should you not become aware of what you have undertaken to do in this lifetime it is not so vitally important. You will know it when you leave this life and then be given the opportunity to make plans and prepare yourself for the next incarnation on earth.

The subordination of spirit and soul to matter which dominates the incarnate sphere is the restriction imposed by natural law and cannot be circumvented. Regardless of your good mediumistic contact to the world beyond, the secrets around you will never be revealed. So do not seek to learn them. It could lead to mistakes with bad consequences.

Be content to take the path ahead of you. Search patiently. Let your actions improve every day. It is not unusual for a person to take the right path and happily bear all its troubles and burdens because he feels and accepts that they are according to natural law and quite just. Despite their worries and sorrows people like this are always cheerful and content. They do not complain about their hard lot and are grateful to be able to do their bit to help mankind. When the majority of incarnate people have progressed to this stage, there will be no restlessness, no discontent, no envy and no hatred in this world.

I cannot describe the other worlds. My spirit and soul are totally earth-orientated. We in the world beyond certainly do not wish to gain insight into other realms. This we are only permitted to do when we have reached a stage of development that lifts us above earthly existence.

My aim is principally to make clear to people how important it really is to allow their spirit and soul to mature in harmony, spare no efforts to develop noble qualities and not persist in the absurd belief that there should be paradise on earth and material possessions to be obtained in abundance without working for them.

Read my explanations over and over again and begin to practise my advice in daily life. Always choose a balance between the two extremes, because even in a positive sense exaggeration is unhealthy as long as matter dominates.

The person who can live completely according to my dictates has not yet been born. This is why I am content with a more moderate approach to these matters.

With this I end the subject of how life's blueprint or programme can be determined and handled. Tomorrow I will deal with other interesting aspects of contact with the fourth dimension.

Aimless wandering of certain spirit entities. Ways of maintaining spiritual contact between the incarnate and discarnate worlds.

IT is time to speak of other matters and clarify certain things which people know too little about. Through their abuse and lack of consideration great harm can come to people on earth and also to souls in the fourth dimension.

It is extremely rare that an entity who leaves incarnate regions is so well informed and prepared that he finds the right path and can get by in the discarnate world.

An ignorant and unprepared spirit entity who enters this world is like a person who comes to a strange country where he doesn't speak the language or know the customs. He wanders around aimlessly without having any idea where to go or what to do, hoping to meet somebody who can help and advise him.

Just as on earth there are endless variations on the theme of wandering around and searching, so there are here. But the conditions are so different from the familiar conditions on earth that the newly arrived spirit entity cannot come to grips with the system to begin with. However, highly developed spirits realise that order does exist here in a measure that is beyond peoples' comprehension.

I must admit that the situation one finds oneself in at first is very confusing. All the more so because death is totally unacceptable. Everybody is convinced that he will recognise this condition, but he doesn't. Rather than wandering around he tries to return to the world he knows where he feels safe and sheltered.

By this I don't mean, and it must not be assumed that every spirit entity wishes to return to earth permanently. It is only immediately after death that he still has an emotional link with the world which he considers so wonderful. Everybody needs a certain time to complete the cross-over.

I have already mentioned that a spirit entity can read the thoughts of people on earth. Now just imagine that a departed spirit, who has not yet recognised his destiny and cannot yet enjoy the splendour of the next world, sees how his family and friends, whom he has left behind, mourn his departure. Naturally he will try to return to them and comfort those who are crying. But he cannot do so. He sees that nobody can hear him. He finds himself in a hopeless situation and desperately casts around for a solution. The stronger his ties are to the material world, the more obstinately he struggles to remain there and ignores all the opinions offered to him as well as the wise counsels of his guide.

As a psychiatrist I was lucky enough to have heard about Spiritualism very often. Even though I rejected closer contact, a part of what I had learned about the link with the infinite remained.

Some people come over in a state of complete ignorance. They are unprepared and unwilling to accept the teachings about continued life in the fourth dimension and recurring incarnations on earth and so on. These individuals have infinite difficulties. It often takes a long time before they adjust to the changes and express the wish to follow a new course.

But the association between the two worlds need not cease. Consequently, mental contact can be maintained with those who have crossed over.

I have already spoken about the power of thought and how it can affect a person who is far away in a positive or negative sense. How much more forcefully will it strike a spirit entity who is no longer held captive in a physical body. Freed from all handicaps and disturbances he will receive thoughts like an antenna.

If your knowledge is advanced and you have deep conviction in the continuity of life, you can send the departed spirit entity your thoughts. You will not be able to establish that contact has been made nor must you expect an answer, but you can be certain that your well-intentioned words and thoughts will, without a doubt reach their destination. You can speak either aloud or in quiet thought. Make him, the newly departed, get used to the idea that he is no longer among people on earth; that he has a new, more advanced way before him and is actually more fortunate than you who are still bound to matter; that he must trust and believe his guides whom Divine

Omnipotence has given him and that good wishes and peaceful thoughts go with him. Tell him his life will continue and he has the opportunity to do all the things that he planned to do on earth, but didn't.

I have already said that there is no God who punishes and takes revenge; who checks the register after death and praises or condemns. A mistake made on earth will not lead to a plunge into hell.

Everybody has the wish to progress, regardless of how little he has until now. He will only remain in the dark until he realises that a life of progress is worth striving for and he has the wish to do so.

Some people choose to make contact with departed spirit entities in seances where materialisation takes place. But this is not in accordance with human nature and must be rejected. Contact through a medium is less sensational, but here too the greatest care must be exercised because what cannot be seen can give rise to error and deception.

Just as people on earth do many things they they should not, so it is here because every spirit entity who crosses over does so at his earthly stage of development.

Furthermore, it depends whether an entity wishes to make contact with the earth immediately after crossing over. I should really say whether he has permission to do so, because every contact from the fourth dimension requires permission from a higher level. My own case is different. I first severed all contact with the incarnate world and then re-established it to do this work.

Meetings arranged between the two worlds that have little value and are only arranged to satisfy curiosity are very seldom allowed. Those who attend such meetings will find their nervous system affected.

If you want to establish contact with a spirit entity and send him positive thoughts, there is no need to summon him to a moving table.

But above all, do not persist in crying and mourning for somebody who has died once you have comforted yourself over the loss. And this should be fairly immediate if you consider that whoever has crossed over has moved into a better life and your tears are only an expression of your sorrow.

I end this chapter with the hope that my explanations about the consequences of separation through death are understandable and acceptable.

MESSSAGES FROM A DOCTOR IN THE FOURTH DIMENSION

Tomorrow we will discuss incarnation and particularly its preconditions.

The course of incarnation.

TODAY I want to describe what happens to a spirit when it reincarnates into the world and what it experiences before crossing over as opposed to what it passes through after earthly death and resurrection into the fourth dimension.

Above all it must be remembered that the discarnate world is the real world. After he has completed his earthly tasks, a person re-enters this life at a higher level than the one he occupied before his last incarnation.

You must accept that what I tell you is according to the knowledge I have been given here and is not based on supposition and belief. Furthermore, I will only pass on information that you can understand.

I have already explained that the spirit entity with all its weaknesses and erroneous opinions, returns to the fourth dimension which is its place of origin.

This can be imagined as a spacious region, although the use of the word "space" can be confusing.

The spirit entity cannot be physically grasped. In earthly language it is called "radiant." It must therefore be apparent that these radiant beings do not require space for their existence.

Remember that the spirit entity does not evolve in the womb and is not inherited from the child's parents. It is a separate entity at its own stage of maturity and enters the body when it has evolved to completion in the womb.

Every mother carrying a child knows that she can determine the various stages of development. She can feel exactly how far the organism has developed, when it makes its first movements and so on.

In an adult or even in a new-born child every movement is directed from the brain. In other words it is an order from the spirit entity and its soul. But the movements in the womb are reflex, caused by impulses from the mother. They are often involuntary and never occasioned by conscious expression but are generated by emotional reflexes. This is understandable as the child in embryo does not move freely within the womb but is bound to the mother by a chord through which it receives all its nourishment and substances for its development.

The moment the chord is freed and cut, there would be a lifeless body if provision had not been made to replace the lost energy. This is the moment of incarnation when the spirit entity enters earthly existence.

Just as the silver chord is ruptured and the release from the material prison is effected when the spirit entity leaves earth, so the procedure is duplicated in the other-worldly sphere when a child is born. Here the spiritual "chord" is in contact with the infinite energies of the cosmos. Once it is broken, the spirit entity loses every recollection of its life in this world. But only the memory, not the state of maturity that it has attained. It must have occurred to you that people who grow up in poor and intellectually inferior surroundings often tower above their fellow men in exceptional measure and display qualities which they could neither have observed nor attracted.

Medical science must continue to build on this important basis. It is quite natural that no mother can follow this process when her child is born. It is apparent that the child is alive when it gives its first cry. In this way the spirit entity shows that it can use its organs and has taken possession of its dwelling place which, in comparison with the freedom offered it in the other world, is very limited.

But this knowledge about the process of incarnation and birth is worthless if it does not teach man to recognise his great responsibility that stems from the task of caring for and promoting a spirit entity on earth. It is the most important commitment that can be undertaken in incarnate existence.

But it is not only an undertaking for parents who have taken the spirit entity into their family circle. It is encumbent on everybody in the community and society to contribute his share of emotional engagement.

Now let us briefly consider what the spirit entity does in the fourth dimension before it incarnates. It is not idle when it is released from the earth but rather pursues its goal further. This, in essence, is achieved by attraction to brighter light. The degree of brightness is according to the level of spiritual maturity already attained.

You no doubt imagine bright light to be brighter at higher levels because on earth, the higher the atmosphere, the brighter the sun shines and it is only dark where there is a cover of some kind over a vantage point. From this comes the concept that spirits live either in higher or lower regions, according to their state of spiritual maturity. The idea does no harm if it is just considered as a point of comparison.

You who are interested in my writings are surely not among the underdeveloped. You are certainly grateful for every pointer given to you that helps you to get closer to the truth and understand the purpose of life. I am happy to assume that you are not materialistic, or at least well on the way to recognising the futility of material possessions.

You will, I hope, move into a brighter sphere when you leave the material world and be able to see the brilliance of much higher ones. Nevertheless, you will immediately realise that you will have to undergo many an earthly test before you can participate in the glories of the cosmos. This realisation will not cause despair, but rather it will make you happy to know that you will be given the opportunity to maintain progress; that the darkness has been overcome and there is only brightness ahead.

In these spheres there is happiness and confidence. Everybody works at putting his energies to good use and cleansing his soul. A long time, in earthly terms, will go by before the very highest decree makes it clear the the time has come to go back to earth if progress is to be maintained. At this stage every spirit knows what awaits it back there. But the time it has to spend on earth is so short in comparison with eternal existence in the discarnate world that it seizes the opportunity with joy and thankfulness in order to be able to work towards the higher development it so ardently desires.

The vast contrast between life in the two worlds has to be clearly understood so that the purpose of creation and its evolution is apparent.

The necessary interdependence between this world and the next.

I HAVE written a lot about what happens when a person enters and then leaves earthly existence. This interesting subject is so difficult to explain because the nature of a spirit entity and matter is radically different and cannot be compared. Yet, like fire and water, which cannot be combined into one substance but nevertheless produce a reciprocal interaction, the spirit entity and the physical body are interdependent.

Every spirit needs another to make progress and achieve perfection. This may be his twin soul. They will not always live together either in this world or the next at the same time. Relationships of this kind therefore exist between the two dimensions and are necessary.

No spirit entity who has found his twin soul and knows that he is on earth will stand by and watch passively and indifferently what happens to him. Just like people who think positive thoughts and send good wishes to beloved children and good friends far away and so influence them for the better, spirit entities are in a position to intervene in earthly lives and help incarnate souls.

This is understandable when you consider how much thought transference gives rise to associations that often cause amazement.

The difference lies in the fact that contacts brought about by thought transference can often be proved later but the influence from the other world cannot. Only people with mediumistic gifts can establish it.

But in my first book I issued a warning and I repeat it now: *without a clear calling and convincing instructions such activity is not to be undertaken.*

Arguments are often raised that mediumistic work, yes, even the reading of mediumistic writings or the wish to learn about beloved persons through a communication are all contrary to the teachings of the Church, but they are not justified.

There are many forms of activity in this sphere that must abolutely be forbidden if mankind, instead of reaping benefits and blessings, is not to bring harm and ruin upon itself.

Centres should be founded which establish whether certain contacts are good or inferior and teach people that association with spirit entities should not be made for pleasure and entertainment.

I must keep repeating this so that readers who are not familiar with the first chapters of my work also get to know it.

Life in the material world has changed in many ways in the course of time. Cultures and civilisations have altered over the centuries. Technical progress has influenced the way of life and will continue to do so in increasing measure in the centuries to come.

Influences emanating from the discarnate world are as old as the material world itself and will exist as long as there are souls on earth who seek ways to develop. There have always been people with mediumistic abilities. Iinvariably, both good and evil spirits have been at pains to intervene in world events, to help and instruct, but also to demolish and destroy.

As long as there are spirit entities who do not live in the spheres of light, there will be conflict and strife, discord and disagreement, in many parts of the world.

I have mentioned that the cosmos is still in a state of fermentation. Not everywhere, but certainly in the incarnate world. Only when matter has been vanquished will there be pure spirituality and the causes of negativity will disappear.

No human being is in a position to assess the time factor needed for this development. In earthly terms it is impossible either to understand or to express such periods of immense duration.

This is why no effort, no matter how small, should be considered futile, even though little progress is apparent. I have said that man carries deep within him the wish and endeavour to attain a higher goal, and that everybody, even he who presently languishes in the dark, will one day find his way into the light.

This is why it is unacceptable that he should resign himself and cease helping others to find the right path. The underlying cause of this is egotism because man requires thanks and recognition for his efforts and considers inner satisfaction of little value. But he should consider his efforts as seeds placed in the ground which require care and only begin to grow after a certain time. The difference lies in the fact that the growth of little spiritual plants need not necessarily begin in this particular earthly existence and the fruits of a good deed and well-meant endeavours are not always harvested by the sower.

So the development of the world, spanning many generations, is influenced by factors whose causes and foundations may stem from bygone eons extending back beyond memory.

All the wisdom available to mankind today in every sphere was already available before the first soul on earth drew breath. The most advanced knowledge is given humanity from infinite sources.

It is left to the personal will of those who benefit from this knowledge to make it available to humanity. If it is used for destruction, mankind will be forced to wait for these benefits in a later existence and will have to battle against material encumbrances all over again.

Let us round off this chapter. Next time we will concern ourselves with matters that are more agreeable and familiar.

Depressions brought on by lack of courage to face oneself and their treatment.

MY aim is to teach people to find the right path on their own and not rely on outside help for every need. Free will should not be interfered with. The decision has often to be made whether to ask advice so that somebody else makes the choice, or to act according to one's own judgement and risk making a mistake.

I have already drawn attention to the fact that an error is an important element on the list of human do's and don'ts. Without it there is no progress because there is no incentive to mobilise your spiritual powers and try to improve. But most people lose heart when they make a mistake. They consider themselves incompetent and forego any effort to progress by happily martyring themselves to their weaknesses. From a psychic point of view such renunciation is dangerous. It generates feelings of inferiority. These in turn lead to resignation and a paralysis of spiritual activity which burdens the soul excessively and diminishes vitality.

People only need the courage to admit their own mistakes. They draw strength from this admission and from the decision to do things differently and better.

Practically all depressions — except those caused by foreign spirit entities which are therefore cases of possession — are vested in this lack of courage.

There are various causes. Principally it results from incorrect education. Parents and teachers, ignorant of the true circumstances, presume that a young person is unable to make independent decisions because such abilities are the exclusive preserve of adults. It is therefore important to apply leverage here so that the future is safeguarded. On an ongoing basis people must be taught to recognise the maturity of the spirit entity. With patience and empathy they must seek to penetrate the psyche of the child to establish whether, and in what measure, it requires support and guidance. It is not the teachers' task to expose and condemn every mistake children make. Their principal duty is to stimulate their pupils to decide themselves whether what they do and think is correct.

Nowadays education cannot function properly without knowledge of the link with the infinite and the Creator's eternal laws.

It would be easy if this knowledge was presented to us on a plate and we were given instructions as to what to do, think and feel. We would not have to make the decisions ourselves, actuate our own wills or take the responsibility for our actions. Taking responsibility means burdening our conscience and criticising what we do and don't do.

A person with a strong will would have no problem making such a decision. And yet every one of us has the same ability. It is incorporated in the programme we bring to earth. When we hesitate and doubt our capacity to make the necessary decisions, we generate uncertainty, dissatisfaction and despondency. The depression, as we call it, is the expression of this condition. There are few people who are free of such emotions and feel confident about the demands made on their conscience, self-control and moral attitude.

Similarly, here in the discarnate world there is not always advanced maturity and recognition or knowledge of the correlations which form the basis of existence. It is often the reverse; total ignorance combined with indifference and disregard for higher values.

People who suffer from depressions are, in the main, more spiritually advanced. The treatment accorded them can proceed on the assumption that external circumstances and events alone are not responsible for the condition. Principally it is caused by the incorrect interpretation of the aim and object of life, the fear of failing and withdrawal from the spiritual level which has already been attained.

In such cases people must be told that their abilities greatly exceed the difficulties they encounter; that their spiritual value is as great as their fellow men's and therefore there is no reason to drift into a condition of resignation.

Depression only comes about when a mistake becomes obvious or truth is not apparent.

It must therefore be possible to cure every depression because when an error is recognised, it is a sign of progress along the upward path.

Not finding truth is an indication that it is being sought and the seeker is already on the road to recovery.

It is apparent to every doctor that such a case does not require medication or an operation, but rather the examination of the patient's mental faculties to pinpoint the blockages hampering their spontaneous activity.

These can be caused by influences from the patient's surroundings or can result from his abnormal emotional attitude.

He is a patient in the true sense of the word and in need of total care and understanding.

Come to think of it, how many people are there who make use of their mental and emotional faculties, who are uninhibited, trusting and unreservedly submit their behaviour to serious and severe scrutiny?

Unfortunately, very few in relation to the tormented and uncertain souls who try to conceal their true natures and present themselves in a different light because they believe them to be offensive or inferior.

Just pay attention and you will see that my words are correct. When once a person accepts the theory that his development hinges on the spiritual standard attained in an earlier life, he will no longer torment himself with self-reproaches and thoughts of inferiority because he knows that everybody has had to go through this or that stage of development.

It is neither a mistake nor a disgrace to belong to those who are less developed. Everybody has a chance to attain perfection and receive his rewards for his efforts.

We must help our fellow beings to find the courage to live, however difficult it may appear to be.

Not only a doctor is designated for this task. Everybody can be a role-model to a fellow human being who is erring around in search of peace and harmony. Show him how, in your own way of life, you have been able to translate into thoughts and deeds your convictions as to what is correct. Correct in the sense of well-being that is not based on self-deception and insincerity but rather on knowledge achieved through honest endeavours and a positive, genuine attitude towards the irrefutable truths.

The topic of fair and equal distribution of possessions to all people should now finally be closed. No power on earth will ever bring about such equality although it would make life healthier if unjustly acquired property was used to compensate for unequally allotted resources.

Dissatisfaction in the material sense will then be abolished once the interactions with the world beyond and the eternal laws become common knowledge. It will still be some time before this is realised, but we want to do our bit in the meantime.

Hysteria, how to recognise and treat it. Negative and positive autosuggestion.

TODAY'S chapter is special. The topic we are going to deal with involves a range of illnesses and handicaps. The diagnosis and subsequent basis for treatment is extremely important.

Often the first abnormal attitudes are only fleeting and brought on through fear of illness or death, but they can also be the cause of an illness.

They are the exaggeration, or inversely, the denial of a pathological condition. The former is more often the case and the doctor then speaks of hysteria or hypochondria. They are the same condition, but according to the sex of the patient either one or other term is applied because of the refusal to believe that a man, like a woman, can be subject to such emotions.

For a long time hysteria was not considered an illness, although its causes were quite natural and understandable; rather, it was considered bad behaviour, attributable in the main to a lack of self-control, self-criticism and self-discipline.

I need not stress that modern science has considerably altered its opinion, but the hypochodriac and the hysteric are still stigmatised. They are considered people who are either feeble or work dodgers with inferiority complexes who take refuge in illness in order to gain the sympathy of the people around them instead of harnessing their energy and willpower to try and attain a seemingly unattainable goal.

No illness is caused by free will for this would contradict the meaning of life. So there must be other causes that give rise to such behaviour.

When they are ill, such people feel themselves cut off from the world. They feel they are unable to have contact with others in the way that those who are healthy do. In order to justify this supposed exclusion to their own conscience, the suffering or pathological condition is exaggerated and presented in a worse light than necessary. It is known that autosuggestion has a very strong influence on the entire organism as well as on the spirit and soul so that it is possible not only to intensify a condition but also actually to bring it on.

It can reach a point where a person cannot eat and induces such organic disorders that his body is in total disarray. If one organ is weak and defenceless, a serious breakdown can result and lead to drastic consequences.

But autosuggestion can also be the greatest help in healing an illness. Indeed, without it the road to recovery can be long and onerous.

Just as a person is obsessed with an idea and cannot let go until he has found the answer to a problem, so such a patient sticks doggedly to his chosen way until he is on the brink of disaster and only fear of death causes him to retrace his steps. He is to be pitied and requires kind and careful treatment administered with endless patience if he is to be cured.

The motives leading to such a predicament are very different and have to be found before treatment can begin.

There is hardly a patient with the correct opinion about his condition, which is why, as I have already said, explanations and descriptions have to be carefully vetted. As soon as he makes an attempt to speak honestly about things, a lot of progress has been made. If he can then be persuaded to examine his situation objectively and prodded into offering moderate self-criticism, the collaboration that will be achieved cannot be highly enough estimated.

It is a different matter with a person who believes, for some reason or other, that he has to lie to himself. This is often quite subconscious. He does not make it easy for the doctor to pinpoint the causes and judge the consequences correctly. Many a patient will express regret that he cannot complete a task he has taken on. In actual fact it is precisely this task that he is running away from, because he doesn't think he is up to it. Illness is then his best refuge because he has not caused it and his failure to complete the work is justified.

But in order to vindicate his behaviour to himself, he really has to make himself feel sick. The first disorders of this kind are, in the main, circulatory problems, followed by bouts of unconsciousness and a collapse of the nervous system. Breathing becomes irregular and the heart function is disturbed. Must not a patient in this condition feel very ill? And does he not warrant the same amount of kindness and loving care as a patient with similar, or the same, physical disturbances? The difference lies only in the fact that the one patient has a sick organ, the other withstands every clinical examination and yet the rhythm of his organ functions is disturbed. Do not make light of his suffering and dismiss it with the thought that the patient is only imagining it. He is often worse off than a patient with an organic illness because he cannot find his way out of his mental and spiritual impasse.

I cannot offer a general cure for such suffering. It is not to be treated with medications. Medications given while the causes are being sought serve as tranquillisers which deaden the pain but do not curb the mental action. Attention must be paid to this. The patient must gradually learn to turn his mind away from what he imagines to be an illness. The best way to lead him back to a normal life is to give him good reading matter, light work and, whenever possible, walks in the fresh air. His energy will increase and so, every day, will his desire for work and achievement. This will not come about if he is given an exaggerated amount of rest and tranquillisers. If the return to normal life is hard at first, the smallest success will be a stimulus and mobilise the will to live so no great effort is required to forget what has gone before. He should be treated with kindness, love, understanding and forgiveness for weaknesses and lapses which are often the reason that a person seeks escape in illness.

Do not underestimate the tasks associated with healing such afflictions. The work is not confined only to the doctor, but extends to everybody who wants to live in harmony with his fellow men. Exaggeration and a lack of honesty are part of a craving for recognition and in extreme cases can bring on illness. What one person overdoes, the next will underplay, according to his spiritual maturity. There is much to say about this aspect of humanity. I will return to it again at a later stage.